# English Word Problems

## 10 Minute Tests

**CEM**

## 10–11+ years

Great Clarendon Street, Oxford, OX2 6DP, United Kingdom

Oxford University Press is a department of the University of Oxford.
It furthers the University's objective of excellence in research, scholarship,
and education by publishing worldwide. Oxford is a registered trade mark
of Oxford University Press in the UK and in certain other countries

Text © Oxford University Press 2017

Author: Michellejoy Hughes

The moral rights of the author have been asserted

First published in 2017

All rights reserved. No part of this publication may be reproduced, stored
in a retrieval system, or transmitted, in any form or by any means, without
the prior permission in writing of Oxford University Press, or as expressly
permitted by law, by licence or under terms agreed with the appropriate
reprographics rights organization. Enquiries concerning reproduction
outside the scope of the above should be sent to the Rights Department,
Oxford University Press, at the address above.

You must not circulate this work in any other form and you must impose
this same condition on any acquirer

British Library Cataloguing in Publication Data
Data available

978-0-19-275938-2

10 9 8 7 6 5

Paper used in the production of this book is a natural, recyclable product
made from wood grown in sustainable forests. The manufacturing process
conforms to the environmental regulations of the country of origin.

Printed in Great Britain by Ashford Colour Ltd.

**Acknowledgements**

Cover illustration: Lo Cole
Illustrations: Aptara
Page make-up: Aptara

The manufacturer's authorised representative in the EU for product safety is
Oxford University Press España S.A. of El Parque Empresarial San Fernando de
Henares, Avenida de Castilla, 2 – 28830 Madrid (www.oup.es/en or product.
safety@oup.com). OUP España S.A. also acts as importer into Spain of
products made by the manufacturer.

# Useful notes

The aim of this book is not to prescribe the exact questions that CEM will produce on an exam paper. CEM do not provide this information and they work from the premise that the format of the questions will change for each exam. The aim of this book is to prepare you for this. There are a variety of question prompts and ways of thinking to extend vocabulary and spelling skills, organised in 10-minute tests.

Use a dictionary and thesaurus to look up unknown words. If you write down each new word, a definition for it and any synonyms or antonyms, it will help extend your vocabulary knowledge. You can keep looking through your words and, when you feel confident, try using them – say them in sentences, write them in your school work or pop them on a whiteboard where you can see them. Make yourself a word-search puzzle or see if someone will test you on the meanings.

There are lots of flashcards available, but you might also like to make your own. Write a word on one side of the card, with as many synonyms as you can find in your thesaurus. You can write the antonym and its synonyms on the back of the card. Now you can test yourself! An alternative version is to write one word on the front of a card and then choose one synonym to write on the front of another card. You can then play 'Pairs' by matching synonyms.

As you work through the book, it is really important that you highlight any questions that you find difficult. *Bond How To Do CEM English and Verbal Reasoning* is a useful subject guide that explains all the question types practised in this book. You can also visit www.bond11plus.co.uk for lots of advice, information and suggestions on everything to do with Bond, the 11+ and helping children to do their best.

The Progress Chart at the back of the book (page 96) is a great way of visualising your progress, and the puzzles are fun activities that will help extend and consolidate word skills.

Keep consolidating the new words that you have learnt, but remember that no exam expects you to know every word or to score 100% in everything. Learning new vocabulary needs to remain an activity that helps you to explore the richness of descriptive words that you can use in your own writing and to help in your comprehension skills. These 10-minute tests are here to challenge you, and to encourage you to think and work quickly.

# Test 1

Test time: 0    5    10 minutes

Find the three-letter word that is needed to complete each word so that each sentence makes sense. Underline the **TWO** answers needed from options **a–e**.

1. The swimming pool had w_____r w_____ed by the sun.

   **a** arm  **b** ale  **c** ate  **d** eat  **e** win

2. My h_____dresser closes on a F_____ay afternoon.

   **a** air  **b** are  **c** red  **d** rid  **e** tin

3. As a t_____nted linguist, he was fluent in six langu_____s.

   **a** ace  **b** age  **c** ale  **d** are  **e** art

4. The cook made a funda_____tal error when he for_____ to add sugar to the cake mixture.

   **a** get  **b** got  **c** gut  **d** man  **e** men

> *Time-saving Tip!*
> You don't have time to write out all possible combinations for these question types, but if you are struggling to decide between one or two options, writing the word out in your own handwriting really helps.

The following sentences all have **ONE** word missing. Complete each sentence by selecting a word from options **a–e**. Underline the correct answer.

5. Mum tried to _____ him to start his homework immediately.

   **a** annoy  **b** wrestle  **c** plead  **d** persuade  **e** infuriate

6. The function room could _____ 200 people comfortably.

   **a** get  **b** seated  **c** invite  **d** standing  **e** accommodate

7. She wanted to be a professional pilot, but she was still an _____.

   **a** amateur  **b** unprofessional  **c** eager  **d** beginner  **e** individual

8   Rose had a guilty _____ because she had copied Ben's work.

    a conscious    b science    c conscience    d confirmed    e think

Select the **ONE** word on the right that has the most **SIMILAR** meaning to the word on the left. Underline the correct answer.

9   enough        a suffering   b sufficient   c insufficient   d scarcity   e indemnity

10  frequently    a rarely      b sometimes    c always         d never      e often

11  pester        a blister     b peel         c harass         d tempt      e sauce

12  vitality      a help        b escape       c wealth         d honour     e vigour

Read the following paragraph and add **ONE** word from the list to each space so that the paragraph makes sense. There are more words than there are spaces so some will be left out, but each word can only be used once.

> also    although    and    by    only    so    was    were

13–16   In September 1666, a dramatic fire began in Pudding Lane in London. Thousands of people _____ left homeless and 80 per cent of London was destroyed. Homes, churches, markets _____ businesses were destroyed, but fortunately _____ six people died. Although the Great Fire of London was a horrendous event, it _____ changed the city by destroying the overcrowded streets that were so full of disease.

# Test 2

Complete the word on the right so that it has the **SAME** or **SIMILAR** meaning to the word on the left.

1  familiarise   | a |   | c |   | s |   | o |   |

2  entrance   | a | d |   |   |   |   |   | n |

3  covert   | u | n |   | e |   | c |   | v |   | r |

4  quiver   | t | r |   |   |   | e |

Underline the **ONE** word on the right that has the most **OPPOSITE** meaning to the word on the left.

5  caution   **a** wariness   **b** raiment   **c** pledge   **d** oppose   **e** recklessness

6  occupy   **a** abandon   **b** correct   **c** immediate   **d** margin   **e** war

7  constant   **a** fluctuating   **b** even   **c** stable   **d** agile   **e** grid

8  follow   **a** drive   **b** sell   **c** forced   **d** guide   **e** light

9  consent   **a** agree   **b** friendly   **c** item   **d** object   **e** firm

10  solid   **a** thorough   **b** curved   **c** sincere   **d** hollow   **e** dark

The following sentences all have a short phrase missing. Complete each sentence by underlining a phrase from options **a–d**.

11  The patient was warned _____ side effects.

   **a** off adverse   **b** of adverse   **c** off averse   **d** of averse

12  The children loved the _____ of the school.

   **a** currant principle   **b** current principle   **c** currant principal   **d** current principal

13  They invited all staff to the meeting _____ workers.

   **a** accept council   **b** accept counsel   **c** except council   **d** except counsel

14  We put the notebook in the _____.

   **a** stationery drawer   **b** stationary drawer   **c** stationery draw   **d** stationary draw

---

Find the missing three letters that complete these words. The three letters do not have to make a word. The same three letters are used for both words.

15  dec_____lisation          gr_____cing

16  n_____ously               eff_____escent

17  gl_____ator               st_____um

18  amphi_____n               pho_____s

19  seri_____ness             th_____ands

20  fas_____ating             medi_____e

# Test 3

Look at the words in the grid and then use them to answer the questions that follow.

| a | archery | b | variety | c | recognise | d | hinder | e | grate |
|---|---|---|---|---|---|---|---|---|---|
| f | obstruct | g | hamper | h | mean | i | breed | j | hospitable |
| k | identify | l | cruel | m | absurd | n | ridiculous | o | gain |
| p | affable | q | accomplish | r | attain | s | lovely | t | know |

1  Find **TWO SYNONYMS** for the word 'friendly'.

_____          _____

2  Find **TWO SYNONYMS** for the word 'achieve'.

_____          _____

3  Find **TWO ANTONYMS** for the word 'sensible'.

_____          _____

4  Find **TWO ANTONYMS** for the word 'help'.

_____          _____

> **Vocabulary Grid Tip!**
> Many descriptive words or verbs will have an opposite. Most nouns won't, unless they have more than one meaning. This can help you to reject some of the words in the grid so that you have fewer to consider.

Find the missing three letters that complete these words. The three letters do not have to make a word. The same three letters are used for both words.

5  f_____ment          f_____rant

6  gregari_____        furi_____ly

7   hyg_____ic           len_____t

8   immed_____ely        pronunc_____ion

Read the following sentences and answer the questions. Underline the most sensible word from options **a–d**.

'The volcano was live and prone to eruptions.'

9   What does the word 'prone' mean in this sentence?

    **a** proved    **b** sending    **c** susceptible    **d** exposed

10  What does the word 'eruptions' mean in this sentence?

    **a** spots    **b** explosions    **c** earthquakes    **d** anger

'After being reprimanded for his behaviour, the boy was repentant.'

11  What does the word 'reprimanded' mean in this sentence?

    **a** schooled    **b** scalded    **c** scolded    **d** scaled

12  What does the word 'repentant' mean in this sentence?

    **a** pleased    **b** proud    **c** annoyed    **d** apologetic

Select the **ONE** word on the right that has the most **SIMILAR** meaning to the word on the left. Underline the correct answer.

13  intrigued    **a** inquisitive    **b** uninterested    **c** trying    **d** encouraged    **e** fallen

14  defective    **a** working    **b** flawless    **c** flaunting    **d** easy    **e** imperfect

15  genuine    **a** unreal    **b** fake    **c** authority    **d** authentic    **e** jewel

16  serious    **a** quiet    **b** busy    **c** hamper    **d** verifiable    **e** solemn

# Test 4

Underline the **ONE** word from options **a–e** that has the most **OPPOSITE** meaning to the word given.

1  profit     a gain       b goods       c loss       d lost       e loose

2  superior   a inferior   b interior    c ulterior   d posterior  e exterior

3  uniform    a same       b different   c neat       d school     e clothes

4  vanished   a polished   b unpolished  c arrive     d absent     e appeared

---

Select the **TWO** odd words out on each line. Select your answers by underlining **TWO** of the options **a–e**.

5  a click    b snap       c break      d chip       e pop

6  a grow     b increase   c enlarge    d minimise   e reduce

7  a nice     b kind       c write      d type       e sort

8  a rotate   b whirl      c turn       d alternative e deal

> **Time-saving Tip!**
> A quick way to solve these questions is to find a connection between any two words. Now go through the other words to see if you can find a third word with the connection. If you can't, try again with another two words.

The following sentences all have **ONE** word missing. Complete each sentence by underlining a word from options **a–e**.

9  The pushy salesman used an _____ sales technique, making him unpopular.

   a upset    b aggressive    c encouraging    d edgy    e independent

10 Mr Gower loved to save money by buying a _____ whenever he could.

   a sale    b inferior    c basement    d present    e bargain

11 The dog's _____ led him into trouble as he would explore dangerous places.

   a tail    b laziness    c curiosity    d humour    e gentleness

12 There was no _____ that the letter would arrive by Tuesday.

   a purpose    b promise    c speed    d sense    e guarantee

> **Word Tip!**
>
> To help you find the right word, it can help to look out for articles. If 'an' is used before a missing word, we know that the missing word begins with a vowel. If 'a' is used, we know that the missing word begins with a consonant.

Select the **ONE** word on the right that has the most **SIMILAR** meaning to the word on the left. Underline the correct answer.

13 illustrate    a significant    b demonstrate    c weak    d poorly    e well

14 nothing    a enough    b nought    c suffering    d helpless    e excessive

15 legendary    a large    b calm    c peaceful    d mythical    e fake

16 moist    a flooded    b arid    c oozing    d damp    e oasis

*Time for a break! ★ Go to Puzzle Page 85 →*

# Test 5

Test time: 0   5   10 minutes

Complete the word on the right so that it has the **SAME** or **SIMILAR** meaning to the word on the left.

1  exciting   | t | h | r |   |   |   |   |   |   |

2  chance    |   |   |   |   |   |   | n | i | t | y |

3  secretive | m |   |   |   |   |   |   | u | s |

4  sickly    | n | a |   |   |   | u | s |

---

The following sentences all have **ONE** word missing. Complete each sentence by underlining a word from options **a–e**.

5  Mrs Smith liked to eat potatoes, _____ Mr Smith preferred pasta.

   **a** but   **b** else   **c** so   **d** because   **e** if

6  The speeding ambulance was responding to a _____ call.

   **a** critic   **b** criticised   **c** critique   **d** cryptic   **e** critical

7  The showroom floor was polished to a high _____ finish.

   **a** matte   **b** gloss   **c** sticky   **d** paint   **e** rough

8  The queen has _____ for many decades.

   **a** led   **b** lead   **c** rained   **d** reigned   **e** reined

Find the missing letters that complete the word on the right so that it has an **OPPOSITE** meaning to the word on the left. Underline the correct answer from options **a–e**.

9  unknown    f __ m __ l __ __ r

    a e e e e    b a e i a    c a i i a    d a i a e    e a i e e

10 tricky    s __ __ __ l i __ __ i __

    a a n d c k c    b p a n n t c    c h a m c k c    d i m p s t c    e i m m s t c

11 rarely    f __ e __ u __ n __ l __

    a r q e t y    b r q i t y    c r c e t y    d r c i t y    e r q a t y

12 problem    s __ l __ t __ o __

    a a t i n    b e l i n    c i a o n    d o u i n    e u a o n

---

Find the missing three letters that complete these words. The three letters do not have to make a word. The same three letters are used for both words.

13  abs_____tely         v_____me

14  appro_____ing        ble_____ed

15  embroi_____ed        thun_____ing

16  co_____geous         nat_____lly

17  frig_____ned         delig_____d

18  sle_____ng           dislo_____ng

# Test 6

Test time: 0  5  10 minutes

These sentences have been jumbled up and all have **ONE** extra word. Underline the word that is not needed.

1  vase in was of the mirror a placed flowers bunch

2  concert the orchestra the school at choir sang

3  on art a midnight has Tuesday class afternoon our

4  neighbour car has our farther a next new door

> *Time-saving Tip!*
>
> A quick way of solving these is to read the words to yourself. Then look away and try to put into words what the sentence is trying to say. Look back again at the words and see if you can put them into order. It should now be easier to find the word that you don't need.

Select the **ONE** word on the right that has the most **OPPOSITE** meaning to the word on the left. Underline the correct answer.

5  available    **a** ready    **b** prepared    **c** absent    **d** present    **e** incapable

6  youthful     **a** young    **b** mature      **c** undeveloped   **d** ripe    **e** pension

7  rural        **a** urban    **b** country     **c** wild      **d** polite    **e** ugly

8  boiling      **a** cool     **b** warm        **c** cold      **d** hot       **e** freezing

Find the missing letters that complete the word on the right so that it has a **SIMILAR** meaning to the word on the left. Underline the correct answer from options **a–e**.

9   pest    n __ __ s __ n __ e

    a  ewas    b  uwas    c  uiec    d  uiac    e  uies

10  habitat    e __ v __ r __ n __ e __ t

    a  niomn    b  naamn    c  niimn    d  noomn    e  niemn

11  relevant    p __ r __ i __ e __ t

    a  atmn    b  atnn    c  etnn    d  etmn    e  otma

12  beats    r __ __ t __ m __

    a  hihs    b  hyhs    c  itas    d  oihs    e  eahs

---

Read the following paragraph and add **ONE** word from the list to each space so that the paragraph makes sense. There are more words than there are spaces so some will be left out, but each word can only be used once.

| a | been | being | both | bought | brought | since | when |

13–16  The astrophysicist Dame Jocelyn Bell Burnell is a specialist in finding radio pulsars. She was _____ up in Northern Ireland and studied at _____ Glasgow and Cambridge universities. At Cambridge, she helped to construct a radio telescope for studying quasars. She held many important scientific posts and in 1999 she was honoured _____ she was appointed Commander of the Order of the British Empire for her services to astronomy. In 2007, she became a Dame and has since _____ listed as one of the 100 most powerful women in the United Kingdom.

# Test 7

Find the three-letter word that is needed to complete each word so that each sentence makes sense. Underline the answer needed from options **a–e**.

1  There was an a_____dance of fruit in the orchard.

   **a** men   **b** bun   **c** can   **d** all   **e** ban

2  The singing competition was an in_____se experience.

   **a** set   **b** and   **c** ten   **d** who   **e** for

3  It was a real privi_____e to meet the world-famous scientist.

   **a** lag   **b** leg   **c** lid   **d** end   **e** saw

4  The little boy was so s_____born he refused to put his coat on.

   **a** win   **b** won   **c** ram   **d** tub   **e** tab

Read the following sentences and answer the questions. Underline the most sensible word from options **a–d**.

'The teaching profession educates a spectrum of ages.'

5  What does the word 'profession' mean in this sentence?

   **a** legal   **b** occupation   **c** people   **d** group

6  What does the word 'spectrum' mean in this sentence?

   **a** young   **b** range   **c** ribbon   **d** ray

'She was bewildered by the lavish decoration around the room.'

7  What does the word 'bewildered' mean in this sentence?

   **a** confused   **b** horrified   **c** repulsed   **d** doubtful

8  What does the word 'lavish' mean in this sentence?

   **a** vile   **b** sickly   **c** extravagant   **d** colourful

Select the **ONE** word on the right that has the most **SIMILAR** meaning to the word on the left. Underline the correct answer.

9   assemble   **a** create   **b** din   **c** pleat   **d** gather   **e** thrust

10  brusque    **a** abrupt   **b** apprehend   **c** able   **d** assist   **e** annoy

11  coarse     **a** study    **b** programme   **c** uneven   **d** smooth   **e** definitely

12  deceive    **a** clown    **b** fool   **c** stupidity   **d** truth   **e** site

13  private    **a** silence  **b** busy   **c** revealed   **d** public   **e** confidential

14  endure     **a** rare     **b** powerful   **c** persist   **d** remove   **e** fade

Select the **TWO** odd words out on each line. Select your answers by underlining **TWO** of the options **a–e**.

15  **a** nervous   **b** calm   **c** edgy   **d** strained   **e** peaceful

16  **a** apple     **b** cherry   **c** lime   **d** grapefruit   **e** lemon

17  **a** acute     **b** sharp   **c** astute   **d** clueless   **e** naive

18  **a** mint      **b** sage   **c** navy   **d** purple   **e** khaki

19  **a** dangerous **b** safe   **c** risky   **d** defenceless   **e** secure

20  **a** dull      **b** drab   **c** vibrant   **d** vivid   **e** radiant

*Time for a break!* ★ *Go to Puzzle Page 86* →

# Test 8

Select the **ONE** word that has the most **OPPOSITE** meaning to the word given. Underline the correct answer from options **a–e**.

1  wasteful    **a** extravagant   **b** lush     **c** litter     **d** thrifty    **e** thriving

2  tranquil    **a** peaceful      **b** wild     **c** biased     **d** quilted    **e** quieten

3  obscure     **a** clean         **b** prevail  **c** plight     **d** clear      **e** fragment

4  liberal     **a** lenient       **b** interesting  **c** boring  **d** caring    **e** intolerant

5  random      **a** erratic       **b** haphazard **c** systematic **d** range     **e** scope

Find the three-letter word that is needed to complete each word so that each sentence makes sense. Underline the **TWO** answers needed from options **a–e**.

6  There was a hot tea_____, milk and sugar on the neat tablec_____h.

   **a** lit    **b** lot    **c** pat    **d** pot    **e** put

7  We sett_____ into our seats to listen to the _____cert.

   **a** con    **b** can    **c** lad    **d** led    **e** lid

8  The arc_____ect studied the _____ustrations thoroughly.

   **a** ail    **b** hat    **c** hit    **d** ill    **e** pun

9  Wild animals need to be p_____ected in their natural ha_____at.

   **a** bat    **b** bit    **c** cat    **d** rut    **e** rot

10 The police were quickly able to appre_____d the thi_____s.

   **a** are    **b** end    **c** eve    **d** fee    **e** hen

Find the missing letters that complete the word on the right so that it has a **SIMILAR** meaning to the word on the left. Underline the correct answer from options **a–e**.

11  devastating   d __ s __ s __ r __ u __

   a aaaos   b eitos   c eatos   d iitos   e iatos

12  owing   o __ __ __ t __ n __ i __ g

   a rsaadn   b shaien   c utsadn   d utsidn   e utsatn

13  brilliant   __ __ __ e l __ e n __

   a speat   b exclt   c exslt   d excit   e exctt

14  plain   __ r d __ n __ r __

   a aeee   b aeey   c oeay   d oiae   e oiay

15  polite   d __ f __ r __ n __ i __ l

   a eeaal   b eeeee   c eaasa   d ealto   e eeeta

Underline the correct words in each of these sentences.

16  We needed to (ensure / insure) our holiday so that we didn't (loose / lose) our money if we had to cancel.

17  Our house has three (stories / storeys), but it is old with lots of (draughts / drafts).

18  Our doctors' (practice / practise) tries not to (proscribe / prescribe) antibiotics to children.

19  A splash of lemon juice really (complements / compliments) the taste of the rich egg (yoke / yolk).

20  We grew wonderful food as the ground used to be (pasta / pasture) land and was so (fertile / futile).

# Test 9

Select the **TWO** odd words out on each line. Select your answers by underlining **TWO** of the options **a–e**.

1   a twist    b twine    c hank    d skein    e ball

2   a metre    b kilogram    c millilitre    d kilometre    e centimetre

3   a boil    b warm    c roast    d bake    e steamy

4   a action    b answer    c respond    d reply    e recite

Underline **ONE** word that is the best fit in each of these sentences.

5   The masked ball was a fabulous event where guests concealed their _____.

   a identities    b dresses    c words    d feelings    e hair

6   Our family had to _____ trips out to save money for our holiday.

   a enjoy    b sacrifice    c spend    d erase    e increase

7   _____ in what we eat is the best way of getting the nutrients we need.

   a Starving    b Snacking    c Drinking    d Monotony    e Variety

8   When she did not hear from him, she was _____ worried.

   a infinitely    b partially    c desperately    d enviously    e independently

Complete the word on the right so that it has an **OPPOSITE** meaning to the word on the left.

9   minimum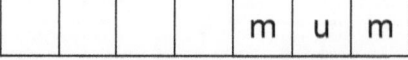

10  strict     | l |   |   |   |   | n | t |

11  unclean    | h |   |   |   |   |   | i | c |

12  old-fashioned | c | o | n |   |   |   |   |   |   | r | y |

> **Letter Tip!**
> If you can't find the word, don't panic! Look at groups of letters and this will help you solve some of it, which may help you find the answer. If you have two consonants together, you are likely to need a vowel next to them. Looking for common groups, such as sh, ch, th, ing, ed, er, dis, con, ary and so on, also might help.

Read the following paragraph and add **ONE** word from the list to each space so that the paragraph makes sense. There are more words than there are spaces so some will be left out, but each word can only be used once.

after   before   into   that   there   therefore   this   under

**13–16** Mr Moseley yawned and stretched. He swung his legs out of bed, placing his feet automatically _____ his comfy pair of slippers, _____ putting on his spectacles. He scratched his chin thoughtfully as it dawned on him _____ it was a Saturday and _____ not a work day. He smiled and stood up before stretching again. Today was going to be a good day.

# Test 10

These sentences have been jumbled up and all have **ONE** extra word. Underline the word that is not needed.

1  inflatables stroke the the played pool on we in swimming

2  tomatoes prefer hot my with I pie custard apple

3  a piano lamp is good my very teacher mum

4  camels have a play rabbits area and our hutch

5  difficult hear is is it music quiet see so the to when

Find the missing letters that complete the word on the right so that it has a **SIMILAR** meaning to the word on the left. Underline the correct answer from options **a–e**.

6  untrue     f __ l __ i __ i __ d
   a acce    b asfe    c acle    d asle    e esfe

7  scary     t e r __ __ f __ __ n g
   a rifi    b ifii    c ifyi    d riyi    e reyi

8  roam      w __ n __ e __
   a odr    b adr    c inr    d idr    e onr

9  remember  r __ c __ l __ e __ t
   a acin    b eoln    c eolc    d oolc    e ooln

10 discourage  d __ s __ __ a __ e
   a esor    b ised    c isud    d esur    e esed

The following sentences all have **ONE** word missing. Complete each sentence by underlining a word from options **a–e**.

**11** The complex case made it _____ for the jury to come to a conclusion.

   **a** possible   **b** difficult   **c** simple   **d** important   **e** irrelevant

**12** The civil war had caused childhood malnutrition through _____ food.

   **a** excess   **b** access   **c** tasteless   **d** sufficient   **e** insufficient

**13** The water cycle looks at how water falls on the land as _____.

   **a** evaporation   **b** sun   **c** precipitation   **d** classification   **e** climate

**14** The cricket ball hit her leg, leaving her sore and _____.

   **a** cut   **b** bruised   **c** grazed   **d** brewed   **e** well

**15** The ring that dangled from the string began to _____ from side to side.

   **a** shine   **b** ascend   **c** oscillate   **d** freeze   **e** titillate

Select the **ONE** word on the right that has the most **OPPOSITE** meaning to the word on the left. Underline the correct answer.

**16** enslaved   **a** liberated   **b** suppressed   **c** enjoyed   **d** sadden   **e** lucid

**17** usual   **a** routine   **b** predictable   **c** familiar   **d** exceptional   **e** plain

**18** vivacious   **a** bright   **b** dull   **c** bubbly   **d** empty   **e** fulfilled

**19** diminish   **a** decline   **b** ascend   **c** descend   **d** increase   **e** plunge

**20** expand   **a** abridge   **b** abound   **c** above   **d** abide   **e** abroad

# Test 11

Find the three-letter word that is needed to complete each word so that each sentence makes sense. Underline the **TWO** answers needed from options **a–e**.

1  I bought a comic and some chocol_____s from the news_____nt's.

   **a** ace   **b** age   **c** ate   **d** eat   **e** out

2  They checked wholes_____ web_____es for the latest prices.

   **a** ail   **b** ale   **c** sat   **d** set   **e** sit

3  The oppo_____ion party had en_____ed with the voting public.

   **a** fag   **b** gag   **c** lit   **d** sit   **e** wit

4  Our lug_____e was packed ready for our va_____ion.

   **a** cat   **b** cot   **c** gag   **d** wag   **e** wig

---

Complete the word on the right so that it has an **OPPOSITE** meaning to the word on the left.

5  serious    | f | r | i |   |   |   |   |   |

6  dull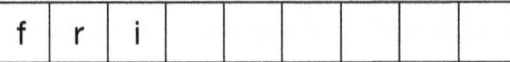

7  inefficient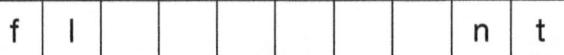

8  wealthy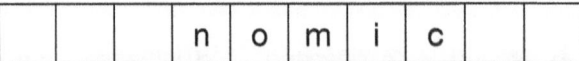

Look at the words in the grid and then use them to answer the questions that follow.

| a debrief | b full | c rowdy | d altitude | e asunder |
| f consideration | g curb | h tardy | i short | j conclude |
| k empty | l humble | m sacred | n unoccupied | o loud |
| p late | q modest | r brief | s noisy | t terminate |

**9** Find **TWO SYNONYMS** for the word 'cease'.

_____     _____

**10** Find **TWO SYNONYMS** for the word 'vacant'.

_____     _____

**11** Find **TWO ANTONYMS** for the word 'conceited'.

_____     _____

**12** Find **TWO ANTONYMS** for the word 'punctual'.

_____     _____

*Word Tip!*

Don't panic if you don't know the word. Try the other questions first and cross out the words that you have already used. If you then need to make an educated guess, try looking for pairs of words.

Underline the correct words in each of these sentences.

**13** The swirling clouds of mist that (envelope / envelop) the open fields make for (adverse / averse) driving conditions.

**14** This was not the best place to remain (stationary / stationery), so we crossed the (desert / dessert) with as much speed as possible.

**15** I could hardly (breath / breathe) after the steep (ascent / assent) to the top of the mountain.

**16** The decorative (freeze / frieze) ran around the weapon room, showing the famous (duels / duals) that the family had won many centuries before.

# Test 12

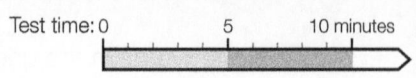

Select the **TWO** odd words out on each line. Select your answers by underlining **TWO** of the options **a–e**.

1. a cute   b sweet   c sour   d bitter   e fashion

2. a see   b observation   c hear   d taste   e show

3. a dense   b thin   c weak   d solid   e impenetrable

4. a exit   b entrance   c hypnotise   d welcome   e mesmerise

5. a careless   b neglectful   c organised   d methodical   e remiss

Select the **ONE** word on the right that has the most **SIMILAR** meaning to the word on the left. Underline the correct answer.

6. determined   a rash   b patient   c keen   d persistent   e sufficient

7. occur   a race   b push   c happen   d try   e magic

8. apparent   a obvious   b hopeless   c awkward   d majestic   e clean

9. system   a machinery   b office   c range   d process   e assortment

10. forbearing   a funny   b patient   c irritated   d intolerant   e moody

> **Word Tip!**
> Sometimes you might have two words that seem equally good. Try thinking of a sentence using the given word. Then try the same sentence again, but this time, replace the word with the other words to see which is the most similar.

Find the missing letters that complete the word on the right so that it has an **OPPOSITE** meaning to the word on the left. Underline the correct answer from options **a–e**.

11  cramped    s __ a __ i __ u __

   a ptos    b psos    c pcos    d ptas    e pcas

12  scarce    p __ e __ t __ f __ l

   a lniu    b rtiu    c rtyu    d lnai    e rsiu

13  frail    f __ r __ i __ i __ d

   a alfe    b utfe    c itfe    d otfy    e otfe

14  built    __ __ m o l __ __ __ e d

   a reliv    b diish    c telir    d deish    e reish

15  previous    s __ b __ e q __ __ n __

   a utuee    b usuat    c utuie    d uuuie    e usuet

Underline the correct words in each of these sentences.

16  The police tried to break up the (hoards / hordes) of angry people to (defuse / diffuse) the situation and to resolve the problem.

17  The (currant / current) method is to treat the bacteria that is causing any (sceptic / septic) infection before it becomes serious.

18  The Water Board planners drew a chalk mark one (meter / metre) away from the (curb / kerb) to indicate where new pipes were to be laid.

19  The children took a (pole / poll) to see which pupils would be chosen to represent them on the school (council / counsel).

20  The (lightening / lightning) process removes, or will (lessen / lesson), colour from a fabric and, in some cases, will return the fabric to its original state.

# Test 13

Underline the **ONE** word on the right that has the most **SIMILAR** meaning to the word given.

1. interrogate    **a** answer    **b** recourse    **c** reply    **d** repose    **e** question

2. extended    **a** abridged    **b** condensed    **c** elongated    **d** curtailed    **e** reduced

3. grave    **a** chart    **b** serious    **c** service    **d** lively    **e** cemetery

4. wholesome    **a** partial    **b** complete    **c** impure    **d** healthy    **e** undue

5. astute    **a** baked    **b** covered    **c** canny    **d** slow    **e** statue

The following sentences all have **ONE** word missing. Complete each sentence by underlining a word from options **a–e**.

6. The office secretary was in charge of the _____ duties.

   **a** administrative    **b** secretly    **c** envelope    **d** adult    **e** junior

7. The crop of stone circles are remnants of an _____ civilisation.

   **a** adhesive    **b** envisage    **c** inferior    **d** exciting    **e** ancient

8. You can't use the Internet in the ward in case it _____ with the equipment.

   **a** fights    **b** interferes    **c** restricts    **d** contracts    **e** contacts

9. She wore unusual clothes that showed her _____ style.

   **a** uniquely    **b** comfort    **c** hair    **d** distinctive    **e** individually

10. There was a shortage of parking so the city charged an _____ fee to park.

    **a** fair    **b** exorbitant    **c** reasonable    **d** competitive    **e** succinct

Find the three-letter word that is needed to complete each word so that each sentence makes sense. Underline the **TWO** answers needed from options **a–e**.

**11** Watching the sun dip_____g below the horizon was hyp_____ic.

    **a** net    **b** not    **c** pan    **d** pin    **e** pun

**12** The simplest _____hods were the most ap_____ling.

    **a** mat    **b** met    **c** pea    **d** sea    **e** tea

**13** Many people use mortg_____s to buy their proper_____s.

    **a** age    **b** are    **c** tap    **d** top    **e** tie

**14** She he_____ated before c_____fully crossing the road.

    **a** are    **b** ore    **c** sat    **d** sit    **e** set

**15** Time had e_____sed between their first s_____ment of stock and this new order.

    **a** hip    **b** hop    **c** lap    **d** top    **e** win

---

Select the **ONE** word on the right that has the most **OPPOSITE** meaning to the word on the left. Underline the correct answer.

**16** nourish     **a** maintain    **b** provide    **c** foster    **d** starve    **e** taste

**17** certain     **a** definite    **b** unsure    **c** reassure    **d** assure    **e** ensure

**18** novice     **a** expert    **b** learner    **c** fresh    **d** cold    **e** perforate

**19** numerous     **a** many    **b** money    **c** digits    **d** grew    **e** few

**20** feasible     **a** achievable    **b** affordable    **c** impossible    **d** refreshed    **e** wise

*Time for a break! ★ Go to Puzzle Page 88 →*

# Test 14

Test time: 0   5   10 minutes

Select the **ONE** word on the right that has the most **OPPOSITE** meaning to the word on the left. Underline the correct answer.

1  embarrassed  **a** nervous  **b** proud  **c** ashamed  **d** annoyed  **e** amazed

2  necessary  **a** vital  **b** wanted  **c** essential  **d** redundant  **e** irregular

3  prejudiced  **a** unbiased  **b** misinformed  **c** mistaken  **d** biased  **e** false

4  recognised  **a** identified  **b** knew  **c** learnt  **d** unfamiliar  **e** suspicious

5  neat  **a** tidy  **b** unkempt  **c** sharp  **d** drone  **e** washed

> **Opposites Tip!**
> Look out for the phrase 'most opposite' in the question. This often indicates that the obvious *exact* opposite is not one of the options. Therefore you must select the *most* opposite from the options given.

These sentences have been jumbled up and all have **ONE** extra word. Underline the word that is not needed.

6  we always eat out when leave room a we candles blow should

7  fog was due a dark storm sky looked as the though

8  the we dog taken walk park took the a for in

9  studying school second country in we the war are world

10  Wales in memorable had family has holidays many have our

Find the missing letters that complete the word on the right so that it has a **SIMILAR** meaning to the word on the left. Underline the correct answer from options **a–e**.

11  rehearse    p __ a __ t __ __ e

   **a** rnin    **b** rsic    **c** rsis    **d** rcic    **e** rcis

12  cooled    c __ i __ __ e __

   **a** lmbd    **b** lnnd    **c** rndd    **d** hlld    **e** hrld

13  rarely    s __ l __ o __

   **a** atn    **b** edm    **c** hom    **d** oom    **e** uln

14  understanding    c __ m __ r __ h __ n __ i __ n

   **a** amgaol    **b** apsiso    **c** opeeso    **d** opeeca    **e** opeesu

15  petty    i __ s __ g n __ f __ c __ n __

   **a** niiiat    **b** nieaat    **c** naaaat    **d** niiiit    **e** niaiat

Underline the correct words in each of these sentences.

16  The artist opened the (drawer / draw) and took out her brushes, paint and mixing (palette / pallet).

17  We need to be (discreet / discrete) if we are to move (foreword / forward) with the surprise party plans.

18  We experienced thunder and (lightening / lightning) before the rain began to (pore / pour).

19  He (passed / past) her a sweet as they stood patiently in the long (cue / queue) at the cinema.

20  I made a list of names that (was / were) too long, so I needed to reduce (it / them) to a more manageable number.

# Test 15

Find the missing three letters that complete these words. The three letters do not have to make a word. The same letters are used for both words.

1  exci_____ent          _____ptation

2  gov_____ment          south_____ers

3  grote_____e           _____eezing

4  inhab_____nts         dig_____l

5  ours_____es           sh_____ing

The following sentences all have a short phrase missing. Complete each sentence by underlining a phrase from options **a–d**.

6  The official gave _____ the whole department.

   **a** advise to   **b** advice to   **c** advise too   **d** advice too

7  Her eyes scanned the supermarket _____ she looked for coconut milk.

   **a** aisle because   **b** isle because   **c** aisle as   **d** isle as

8  With _____, we watched in amazement at the scene.

   **a** baited breathe   **b** baited breath   **c** bated breath   **d** bated breathe

9  Did the tree's _____ during the storm or was it cut on purpose?

   **a** bow brake   **b** bough brake   **c** bow break   **d** bough break

10 We _____ the two arches that spanned the river.

   **a** sailed among   **b** sail among   **c** sailing between   **d** sailed between

Underline the **ONE** word on the right that has the most **SIMILAR** meaning to the word given.

11  release   a relief   b restrain   c restart   d resolve   e resign

12  trivial   a heavy   b vitality   c insignificant   d boring   e pursuit

13  ordeal   a perfect   b affliction   c sequence   d fun   e comfort

14  seize   a large   b smaller   c shove   d push   e snatch

15  fleck   a soot   b spot   c stop   d bendy   e rigid

---

Select the **ONE** word on the right that has the most **OPPOSITE** meaning to the word on the left. Underline the correct answer.

16  extend   a increase   b estate   c shrink   d lengthen   e stress

17  below   a under   b above   c between   d with   e beneath

18  forget   a misplace   b omit   c remember   d restore   e regain

19  casual   a permanent   b flippant   c for   d think   e indifferent

20  bold   a bald   b aged   c dark   d timid   e tirade

# Test 16

Select the **ONE** word on the right that has the most **SIMILAR** meaning to the word on the left. Underline the correct answer.

1. mischievous   **a** magical   **b** evil   **c** playful   **d** tricky   **e** cool

2. category   **a** kit   **b** group   **c** equipment   **d** sense   **e** title

3. accompany   **a** escort   **b** loneliness   **c** company   **d** friendship   **e** duo

4. controversy   **a** contrived   **b** debate   **c** poetry   **d** forced   **e** loved

5. gorge   **a** fleece   **b** flight   **c** mountain   **d** ravine   **e** sea

Select the **TWO** odd words out on each line. Select your answers by underlining **TWO** of the options **a–e**.

6. **a** rain   **b** wind   **c** rotate   **d** turn   **e** hot

7. **a** fair   **b** unjust   **c** pale   **d** heavy   **e** light

8. **a** revenge   **b** retaliation   **c** retribution   **d** innocent   **e** unblemished

9. **a** found   **b** fund   **c** head   **d** back   **e** sponsor

10. **a** pound   **b** pence   **c** pummel   **d** thump   **e** sense

### Word Tip!

Sometimes it is difficult to find any connection, so take the first word in the list and see how many meanings there are of the word. Many words are homonyms and this might help you find a connection.

The following sentences all have **ONE** word missing. Complete each sentence by underlining a word from options **a–e**.

11  After the funeral, family and friends left flowers at the _____.

   **a** symmetry   **b** sincerely   **c** commentary   **d** civilly   **e** cemetery

12  At the village hall, there was a meeting about local _____.

   **a** concerns   **b** corners   **c** complications   **d** regales   **e** affections

13  The film was shown on the largest cinema _____.

   **a** viewers   **b** room   **c** auditorium   **d** screen   **e** projection

14  Isaac can't run in the race as he has pulled a _____ in his leg.

   **a** mussel   **b** muscle   **c** muzzle   **d** muddle   **e** ankle

These sentences have been jumbled up and all have **ONE** additional word. Select the extra word in each of the sentences by underlining **ONE** word from options **a–e**.

15  swam on sea the man the edge looking stood cliff out to

   **a** cliff   **b** looking   **c** sea   **d** stood   **e** swam

16  the green lights stopped waiting because to turn them for car at the

   **a** because   **b** car   **c** lights   **d** stopped   **e** waiting

17  book closed get excited was present opened I my and so to the

   **a** book   **b** closed   **c** excited   **d** present   **e** the

18  warm it keep was to so scarf cold winter and we hat put gloves on our

   **a** cold   **b** gloves   **c** scarf   **d** warm   **e** winter

# Test 17

Look at the words in the grid and then use them to answer the questions that follow.

| a spoil | b commence | c colour | d neat | e basic |
|---|---|---|---|---|
| f ambition | g dishevelled | h error | i begin | j beck |
| k completely | l mistake | m mere | n residence | o damage |
| p untidy | q device | r abode | s burden | t uncomplicated |

1  Find **TWO SYNONYMS** for the word 'ruin'.

   _____      _____

2  Find **TWO SYNONYMS** for the word 'dwelling'.

   _____      _____

3  Find **TWO ANTONYMS** for the word 'complex'.

   _____      _____

4  Find **TWO ANTONYMS** for the word 'neat'.

   _____      _____

> *Pairing Tip!*
> Try pairing up the words in the grid so that you can reduce the number of meanings. Cross out any words that don't match with another as you go. Then try each pair against the questions to see if any fit.

These sentences have been jumbled up and all have **ONE** extra word. Underline the word that is not needed.

5  never angrily look at you sun the must directly

6  bigger small kaleidoscope microscope makes a things appear

**7** favourite is chips my on toast breakfast jam

**8** six had cat of fluffy has our kittens

---

Select the **ONE** word on the right that has the most **OPPOSITE** meaning to the word on the left. Underline the correct answer.

**9** leisure    **a** work    **b** hobby    **c** sport    **d** rest    **e** test

**10** amateur    **a** pretend    **b** rough    **c** precise    **d** professional    **e** substandard

**11** attached    **a** with    **b** constricted    **c** separated    **d** thatched    **e** involved

**12** mock    **a** practise    **b** praise    **c** pretend    **d** precise    **e** preview

---

Find the three-letter word that is needed to complete each word so that each sentence makes sense. Underline the answer needed from options **a–e**.

**13** We caught a gl_____se of the sea through the trees.

   **a** imp    **b** and    **c** end    **d** are    **e** ere

**14** School-trip places are allo_____ed on a strictly first come, first served basis.

   **a** cab    **b** cad    **c** car    **d** cat    **e** cay

**15** We were st_____gling to get our suitcases into the taxi.

   **a** rub    **b** rug    **c** are    **d** ire    **e** ore

**16** That was definitely the s_____iest story I have ever read!

   **a** par    **b** ten    **c** war    **d** tar    **e** car

# Test 18

Find the three-letter word that is needed to complete each word so that each sentence makes sense. Underline the **TWO** answers needed from options **a–e**.

1 He always _____ried a mirror to check his ap_____rance.

   **a** car   **b** far   **c** mar   **d** pea   **e** ear

2 The animal was hunted to ex_____ction by poac_____s.

   **a** tan   **b** tin   **c** him   **d** her   **e** our

3 The pr_____less ring contained a f_____less diamond.

   **a** ace   **b** ice   **c** law   **d** low   **e** raw

4 After their ar_____ent, the two boys were now sub_____d.

   **a** rib   **b** rub   **c** gem   **d** gum   **e** due

Read the following sentences and answer the questions. Underline the most sensible word from options **a–d**.

'Contribute what you can afford and we will be able to raise the money.'

5 What does the word 'contribute' mean in this sentence?

   **a** spend   **b** save   **c** donate   **d** do

6 What does the word 'raise' mean in this sentence?

   **a** lift   **b** collect   **c** spend   **d** decline

'Even with the many objections, halting progress was impossible.'

7 What does the word 'objections' mean in this sentence?

   **a** protests   **b** compliments   **c** items   **d** injections

8 What does the word 'halting' mean in this sentence?

   **a** hearing   **b** finding   **c** starting   **d** stopping

# Answers

## Test 1

1  **c** ate, **a** arm (The swimming pool had water warmed by the sun.)
2  **a** air, **d** rid (My hairdresser closes on a Friday afternoon.)
3  **c** ale, **b** age (As a talented linguist, he was fluent in six languages.)
4  **e** men, **b** got (The cook make a fundamental error when he forgot to add sugar to the cake mixture.)
   'Forgot' is correct because it is in the past tense.
5  **d** (Mum tried to **persuade** him to start his homework immediately.)
6  **e** (The function room could **accommodate** 200 people comfortably.)
7  **a** (She wanted to be a professional pilot, but she was still an **amateur**.)
   'Amateur' means 'not professional' and it goes with the indefinite article (which 'beginner' does not).
8  **c** (Rose had a guilty **conscience** because she had copied Ben's work.)
   'Guilty conscience' tells us that someone knows they have done something wrong.
9  **b** sufficient
   'Insufficient' and 'scarcity' have opposite meanings.
10  **e** often
   'Rarely', 'sometimes' and 'never' mean something occurs less than 'often'.
11  **c** harass
12  **e** vigour
13–16  (13) were: 'thousands of people' is plural.
   (14) and: 'businesses' is the last noun in a list.
   (15) only: emphasises that the number of people who died was low.
   (16) also: indicates that we are about to read about another effect of the Great Fire.

## Test 2

1  accustom
2  admission
3  undercover
4  tremble
5  **e** recklessness
   'Wariness' has a similar meaning to 'caution'.
6  **a** abandon
   If you 'occupy' a building, you live in it. If you 'abandon' a building, you leave or vacate it.
7  **a** fluctuating
   'Even' and 'stable' both have similar meanings to 'constant'.
8  **d** guide
   The word 'guide' can be a verb. For example, 'I will guide you and you can follow me.'
9  **d** object
   'Consent' can mean 'to agree' to something. 'Object' can mean 'to disagree'.
10  **d** hollow
   'Solid' can mean 'dense' or 'filled the whole way through'. 'Hollow' can mean there is nothing in the centre, just an outside shell.
11  **b** (The patient was warned **of adverse** side effects.)
   The word 'warn' is usually followed by the preposition 'of' or 'about', and 'adverse' means 'harmful', while 'averse' means 'unwilling'.
12  **d** (The children loved the **current principal** of the school.)
   Here, 'current' means 'present' or 'in post', while 'currant' is a fruit. It is easy to confuse 'principle' and 'principal', but remember it by thinking that a princi**pal** (head teacher) is your pal.
13  **c** (They invited all staff to the meeting **except council** workers.)
   'Except' means 'not including'. 'counsel' means 'advice' (noun) or 'to advise' (verb), so is not correct.

**14 a** (We put the notebook in the **stationery drawer**.)

To learn the difference between 'stationery' and 'stationary', remember that a letter (which has two '**e**'s) is station**e**ry; and something that is 'station**a**ry' st**a**ys.

**15** ima (decimalisation, grimacing)

**16** erv (nervously, effervescent)

**17** adi (gladiator, stadium)

**18** bia (amphibian, phobias)

**19** ous (seriousness, thousands)

**20** cin (fascinating, medicine)

## Test 3

**1 j** hospitable, **p** affable

Someone who is 'friendly' is 'hospitable' and 'affable'.

**2** Any two of: **o** gain, **q** accomplish, **r** attain

These words can all mean 'complete' or 'succeed' in something.

**3 m** absurd, **n** ridiculous

Both 'absurd' and 'ridiculous' mean 'unreasonable' or 'illogical'.

**4** Any two of: **d** hinder, **f** obstruct, **g** hamper

'Hinder', 'hamper' and 'obstruct' can all mean 'prevent someone from doing something'.

**5** rag (fragment, fragrant)

**6** ous (gregarious and furiously)

**7** ien (hygienic and lenient)

**8** iat (immediately and pronunciation)

**9 c** susceptible

Both 'prone' and 'susceptible' mean 'liable'.

**10 b** explosions

In a volcanic eruption, lava and other material explode out of the volcano.

**11 c** scolded

Both 'reprimanded' and 'scolded' mean 'told off'.

**12 d** apologetic

If someone is 'repentant', they are 'regretful' and 'apologetic'.

**13 a** inquisitive

'Uninterested' has an opposite meaning.

**14 e** imperfect

'Flawless' has an opposite meaning.

**15 d** authentic

'Unreal' and 'fake' have opposite meanings.

**16 e** solemn

## Test 4

**1 c** loss

'Loss' is a better choice than 'lost' because 'loss' and 'profit' are both nouns.

**2 a** inferior

Both 'inferior' and 'superior' refer to position or quality ('lower' and 'higher').

**3 b** different

'Same' has a similar meaning to 'uniform'; 'clothes' has a similar meaning to 'uniform' in the sense of dress code.

**4 e** appeared

'Appeared' is a better choice because it is in the past tense, while 'arrive' is in the present tense.

**5 a** click, **e** pop

'Snap', 'break' and 'chip' all mean 'to damage'.

**6 d** minimise, **e** reduce

'Grow', 'increase' and 'enlarge' all mean 'make larger'.

**7 a** nice, **c** write

'Kind', 'type' and 'sort' all mean 'category'.

**8 d** alternative, **e** deal

'Rotate', 'whirl' and 'turn' all mean 'spin'.

**9 b** (The pushy salesman used an **aggressive** sales technique, making him unpopular.)

'Aggressive' means 'forceful' in a negative way.

**10 e** (Mr Gower loved to save money by buying a **bargain** whenever he could.)

'Bargain' means 'something cheap'.

**11 c** (The dog's **curiosity** led him into trouble as he would explore dangerous places.)

'Curiosity' means 'inquisitiveness'.

**12 e** (There was no **guarantee** that the letter would arrive by Tuesday.)

'Guarantee' means that something has been agreed. It is more official than 'promise'.

13 **b** demonstrate

14 **b** nought

'Nought' can mean 'nothing' – much less than 'sufficient'. 'Excessive' means 'much more than necessary' – more than 'sufficient'.

15 **d** mythical

'Legendary' and 'mythical' can both be used to describe things that are not true but are widely held to be true in some sense, while 'fake' simply means 'not genuine'.

16 **d** damp

'Damp' is a better choice than 'oozing' because 'oozing' means that liquid is leaking out, while 'damp' and 'moist' do not imply this.

## Test 5

1 thrilling
2 opportunity
3 mysterious
4 nauseous
5 **a** (Mrs Smith liked to eat potatoes, **but** Mr Smith preferred pasta.)

'But' is a conjunction used to introduce contrast, such as different point of view, as here.

6 **e** (The speeding ambulance was responding to a **critical** call.)

'Critical' is an adjective meaning 'serious' or 'life-threatening'.

7 **b** (The showroom floor was polished to a high **gloss** finish.)

'Gloss' is correct because it means 'shiny'.

8 **d** (The queen has **reigned** for many decades.)

'Reigned' is correct because it means 'ruled'.

9 **c** a i i a (familiar)

'Familiar' means 'known'.

10 **d** i m p s t c (simplistic)

'Simplistic' means 'excessively simple'.

11 **a** r q e t y (frequently)

'Frequently' means 'often'.

12 **d** o u i n (solution)

A 'solution' can be used to solve a problem.

13 olu (absolutely, volume)
14 ach (approaching, bleached)
15 der (embroidered, thundering)
16 ura (courageous, naturally)
17 hte (frightened, delighted)
18 dgi (sledging, dislodging)

## Test 6

1 mirror (The bunch of flowers was placed in a vase OR A bunch of flowers was placed in the vase.)
2 orchestra (The school choir sang at the concert.)
3 midnight (Our class has art on a Tuesday afternoon.)
4 farther (Our next door neighbour has a new car OR Our new next door neighbour has a car.)
5 **c** absent
6 **b** mature

'Mature' is a better choice than 'ripe' because 'youthful' and 'mature' usually describe people. 'Ripe' is usually used to describe fruit.

7 **a** urban

'Country' and 'wild' both have similar meanings to 'rural'.

8 **e** freezing

'Freezing' is a better choice than 'cold' because both 'freezing' and 'boiling' describe extreme temperatures.

9 **d** u i a c (nuisance)
10 **a** n i o m n (environment)
11 **c** e t n n (pertinent)
12 **b** h y h s (rhythms)

13–16 **(13)** brought: 'brought up' is the past tense of 'bring up'.

**(14)** both: indicates that Dame Jocelyn studied at two universities.

**(15)** when: used as an adjective to describe the time at which Dame Jocelyn was honoured.

**(16)** been: 'has been listed' tells us that others have ranked her as one of the UK's most powerful women.

## Test 7

1. **b** bun (There was an abundance of fruit in the orchard.)
2. **c** ten (The singing competition was an intense experience.)
3. **b** leg (It was a real privilege to meet the world-famous scientist.)
4. **d** tub (The little boy was so stubborn he refused to put his coat on.)
5. **b** occupation

   Both 'occupation' and 'profession' are used to describe what someone does to earn a living.
6. **b** range

   Both 'range' and 'spectrum' can be used to describe a variety of ages, from very young to very old.
7. **a** confused

   If someone is 'bewildered', they are 'confused', 'puzzled' or 'baffled'.
8. **c** extravagant

   Both 'extravagant' and 'lavish' mean 'generous', 'abundant'.
9. **d** gather

   'Assemble' is a verb so 'din' (noun) is not a viable synonym.
10. **a** abrupt

    'Brusque' is an adjective, but 'apprehend', 'assist' and 'annoy' are verbs.
11. **c** uneven

    'Smooth' has an opposite meaning, and 'study', 'programme' and 'definitely' have completely different meanings, although 'study' and 'programme' are similar to the homophone 'course'.
12. **b** fool

    In this case, 'fool' is used as a verb with a similar meaning to 'deceive'. 'Clown' has a similar meaning to 'fool' when that word is used as a noun.
13. **e** confidential

    'Confidential' and 'private' can both mean 'to be secret'.
14. **c** persist

    'Persist' and 'endure' can both mean 'to continue'.
15. **b** calm, **e** peaceful

    'Nervous', 'edgy' and 'strained' can all be used to describe someone who is feeling tense or worried.
16. **a** apple, **b** cherry

    All the words are fruits, but 'lime', 'grapefruit' and 'lemon' are all citrus fruits.
17. **d** clueless, **e** naïve

    'Acute', 'sharp' and 'astute' can all mean 'perceptive'.
18. **c** navy, **d** purple

    All the words are colours, but 'mint', 'sage' and 'khaki' are all shades of green.
19. **b** safe, **e** secure

    'Dangerous', 'risky' and 'defenceless' all mean 'to be unprotected'.
20. **a** dull, **b** drab

    'Vibrant', 'vivid' and 'radiant' all mean 'colourful' and 'rich'.

## Test 8

1. **d** thrifty

   'Extravagant' has a similar meaning to 'wasteful', and 'lush', 'litter' and 'thriving' have completely different meanings.
2. **b** wild

   'Peaceful' has a similar meaning to 'tranquil', as does 'quieten', although 'quieten' is a verb, not an adjective. 'Biased' and 'quilted' have completely different meanings.
3. **d** clear

   'Obscure' can mean 'not clear', 'dim' and 'dark' so the word 'clear' is the best fit.
4. **e** intolerant

   A 'liberal' person is open-minded, while an 'intolerant' person does not tolerate opinions or behaviour different from their own.
5. **c** systematic

   'Random' can mean 'erratic' and 'without planning'. 'Systematic' can mean 'carefully planned'.
6. **d** pot, **b** lot (There was a hot teapot, milk and sugar on the neat tablecloth.)
7. **d** led, **a** con (We settled into our seats to listen to the concert.)

8  **c** hit, **d** ill (The architect studied the illustrations thoroughly.)

9  **e** rot, **b** bit (Wild animals need to be protected in their natural habitat.)

10 **e** hen, **c** eve (The police were quickly able to apprehend the thieves.)

11 **e** i a t o s (disastrous)

Both 'disastrous' and 'devastating' mean 'terrible'.

12 **c** u t s a d n (outstanding)

Both 'outstanding' and 'owing' can mean that something is yet to be paid or returned.

13 **b** e x c l t (excellent)

Both 'excellent' and 'brilliant' mean 'wonderful'.

14 **e** o i a y (ordinary)

Both 'ordinary' and 'plain' mean 'unremarkable'.

15 **e** e e e t a (deferential)

'Polite' and 'deferential' both mean 'to be courteous'.

16 We needed to **insure** our holiday so that we didn't **lose** our money if we had to cancel.

'Insure' means 'to buy insurance'.

17 Our house has three **storeys**, but it is old with lots of **draughts**.

A 'storey' is a floor of a building. A 'draught' is a current of air.

18 Our doctors' **practice** tries not to **prescribe** antibiotics to children.

'Practice' is the noun form, rather than the verb form (practise). 'Prescribe' can mean 'advise the use of medicine' (think of 'prescription').

19 A splash of lemon juice really **complements** the taste of the rich egg **yolk**.

'Complements' means 'completes' and is often used in the sense of 'goes well with' or 'enhances'. 'Yolk' is the yellow part of an egg.

20 We grew wonderful food as the ground used to be **pasture** land and was so **fertile**.

'Pasture' is land that animals have grazed on. 'Fertile' means it is able to grow crops.

# Test 9

1  **a** twist, **b** twine

'Hank', 'skein' and 'ball' can all be used to describe a quantity of wool.

2  **b** kilogram, **c** millilitre

'Metre', 'kilometre' and 'centimetre' are all units of length.

3  **b** warm, **d** steamy

'Boil', 'roast' and 'bake' are all cooking methods.

4  **a** action, **d** recite

'Answer', 'respond' and 'reply' all mean the same.

5  **a** (The masked ball was a fabulous event where guests concealed their **identities**.)

'A masked ball' is a dance at which guests all wear masks to cover their faces.

6  **b** (Our family had to **sacrifice** trips out to save money for our holiday.)

'Sacrifice' means 'to give up'.

7  **e** (**Variety** in what we eat is the best way of getting the nutrients we need.)

'Variety' means 'diversity' – eating lots of different foods means we get different nutrients.

8  **c** (When she did not hear from him, she was **desperately** worried.)

'Desperately' describes what level of worry was experienced. 'Infinitely' and 'partially' can also be used to describe the level of something, but it would be unusual to say 'infinitely worried' or 'partially worried'.

9  maximum

10 lenient

11 hygienic

12 contemporary

13–16 **(13)** into: a preposition expressing direction of movement. Mr Moseley is more likely to put his feet 'into' his slippers than 'under' them.

**(14)** before: a conjunction used to describe the sequence of events. It is a better choice than 'after' because it is more likely that Mr Moseley would put on his slippers immediately after swinging his legs out of bed, and therefore 'before' putting on his spectacles.

**(15)** that: used to introduce the defining clause that tells us what Mr Moseley realised.

**(16)** therefore: an adverb meaning 'for that reason'.

## Test 10

1. stroke (We played on the inflatables in the swimming pool.)
2. tomatoes (I prefer hot custard with my apple pie OR I prefer my apple pie hot with custard.)
3. lamp (My mum is a very good piano teacher.)
4. camels (Our rabbits have a hutch and play area OR Our rabbits have a play area and hutch.)
5. see (It is difficult to hear when the music is so quiet.)
6. **b** a s f e (falsified)

   If something has been 'falsified' it is 'untrue'.
7. **d** r i y i (terrifying)

   Both 'terrifying' and 'scary' mean 'frightening'.
8. **b** a d r (wander)

   Both 'wander' and 'roam' mean 'ramble' or 'travel unsystematically'.
9. **c** e o l c (recollect)

   Both 'remember' and 'recollect' mean 'to think about something that happened in the past'.
10. **c** i s u d (dissuade)

    'Discourage' and 'dissuade' both mean 'to try to prevent something from happening'.
11. **b** (The complex case made it **difficult** for the jury to come to a conclusion.)

    'Difficult' means 'challenging'.
12. **e** (The civil war had caused childhood malnutrition through **insufficient** food.)

    'Insufficient' means 'not enough', and 'malnutrition' tells us the children weren't getting enough nutrients from their food.
13. **c** (The water cycle looks at how water falls on the land as **precipitation**.)

    'Precipitation' means 'rainfall'.
14. **b** (The cricket ball hit her leg, leaving her sore and **bruised**.)

    A bruise is the most likely result of being hit.
15. **c** (The ring that dangled from the string began to **oscillate** from side to side.)

    The word 'oscillate' means to swing.
16. **a** liberated

    'Suppressed' has a similar meaning, and 'enjoyed', 'sadden' and 'lucid' all have completely different meanings.
17. **d** exceptional

    'Routine', 'predictable' and 'familiar' have similar meanings, and 'plain' has a different meaning.
18. **b** dull

    'Bright' and 'bubbly' have similar meanings to 'vivacious', and 'empty' and 'fulfilled' have completely different meanings.
19. **d** increase

    'Decline' can have a similar meaning, and 'ascend', 'descend' and 'plunge' have different meanings.
20. **a** abridge

    'Expand' means 'to make larger'. 'Abridge' means 'to shorten' something.

## Test 11

1. **c** ate, **b** age (I bought a comic and some chocolates from the newsagent's.)
2. **b** ale, **e** sit (They checked wholesale websites for the latest prices.)
3. **d** sit, **b** gag (The opposition party had engaged with the voting public.)
4. **c** gag, **a** cat (Our luggage was packed ready for our vacation.)
5. frivolous
6. flamboyant
7. economical
8. destitute
9. **j** conclude, **t** terminate

   Both mean 'bring to an end', or 'cease'.
10. **k** empty, **n** unoccupied

    A 'vacant' house is 'empty' and 'unoccupied'.
11. **l** humble, **q** modest

    Both 'humble' and 'modest' can mean 'having a low opinion of oneself'.
12. **h** tardy, **p** late

    Both mean 'delayed' or 'not on time'.
13. The swirling clouds of mist that **envelop** the open fields make for **adverse** driving conditions.

    'Envelop' means 'to cover completely'. 'Adverse' means 'harmful' or 'hostile'.

14  This was not the best place to remain **stationary**, so we crossed the **desert** with as much speed as possible.

'Stationary' means 'still, unmoving' (while 'stationery' relates to writing materials). 'Desert' means 'a barren, dry area of land'.

15  I could hardly **breathe** after the steep **ascent** to the top of the mountain.

'Breathe' is the verb form. 'Ascent' means 'route by which you can ascend'.

16  The decorative **frieze** ran around the weapon room, showing the famous **duels** that the family had won many centuries before.

A 'frieze' is a band of decoration. A 'duel' is a contest between two people.

## Test 12

1  **a** cute, **e** fashion

'Sweet', 'sour' and 'bitter' all relate to taste.

2  **b** observation, **e** show

'See', 'hear' and 'taste' are all senses.

3  **b** thin, **c** weak

'Dense', 'solid' and 'impenetrable' can all be used to describe something thick or impassable.

4  **a** exit, **d** welcome

'Entrance', 'hypnotise' and 'mesmerise' can all mean 'put someone in a trance'.

5  **c** organised, **d** methodical

'Careless', 'neglectful' and 'remiss' all mean 'negligent' or 'slapdash'.

6  **d** persistent

'Keen', meaning 'eager', is similar, but doesn't imply stubbornness as both 'persistent' and 'determined' do.

7  **c** happen

8  **a** obvious

9  **d** process

Both 'process' and 'system' mean 'procedure' or 'routine'.

10  **b** patient

'Forbearing' can mean 'to be patient'.

11  **c** p c o s (spacious)

'Spacious' means 'roomy'.

12  **a** l n i u (plentiful)

'Plentiful' means 'ample' or 'abundant'.

13  **e** o t f e (fortified)

'Fortified' means 'made strong'.

14  **d** d e i s h (demolished)

'Demolished' means 'destroyed' or 'violently taken apart'.

15  **e** u s u e t (subsequent)

'Subsequent' refers to what follows next. 'Previous' refers to what came before.

16  The police tried to break up the **hordes** of angry people to **defuse** the situation and to resolve the problem.

'Hordes' means 'crowds'. 'Defuse' means 'to reduce the tension or danger'.

17  The **current** method is to treat the bacteria that is causing any **septic** infection before it becomes serious.

'Current' means 'present' or 'in use'. 'Septic' means 'contaminated with bacteria'.

18  The Water Board planners drew a chalk mark one **metre** away from the **kerb** to indicate where new pipes were to be laid.

'Metre' is a unit of length. 'Kerb' is a noun meaning 'the edge of a pavement'.

19  The children took a **poll** to see which pupils would be chosen to represent them on the school **council**.

'Poll' means 'vote'. 'Council' means 'a body of people', in this case representing the school's pupils.

20  The **lightening** process removes, or will **lessen**, colour from a fabric and, in some cases, will return the fabric to its original state.

'Lightening' is to make something lighter and, 'lessen' is to make less of something.

## Test 13

1  **e** question

'Answer' and 'reply' have opposite meanings, and 'recourse' and 'repose' have completely different meanings.

**2 c** elongated

The other four options all have opposite meanings to 'extended'.

**3 b** serious

'Cemetery' has a similar meaning to 'graveyard', but not to 'grave'.

**4 d** healthy

'Complete' is similar to 'whole' but not to 'wholesome'.

**5 c** canny

'Canny' and 'astute' both mean 'shrewd' and 'wise'.

**6 a** (The office secretary was in charge of the **administrative** duties.)

Administration is part of a secretary's role.

**7 e** (The crop of stone circles are remnants of an **ancient** civilisation.)

'Ancient' is the best choice here because 'remnants' means 'things left over' and tells us that the stone circles are very old.

**8 b** (You can't use the Internet in the ward in case it **interferes** with the equipment.)

'Interferes' means 'affects in an undesirable way'.

**9 d** (She wore unusual clothes that showed her **distinctive** style.)

'Distinctive' means 'characteristic' or 'individual'.

**10 b** (There was a shortage of parking so the city charged an **exorbitant** fee to park.)

'Exorbitant' means excessively expensive.

**11 d** pin, **b** not (Watching the sun dipping below the horizon was hypnotic.)

**12 b** met, **c** pea (The simplest methods were the most appealing.)

**13 a** age, **e** tie (Many people use mortgages to buy their properties.)

**14 d** sit, **a** are (She hesitated before carefully crossing the road.)

**15 c** lap, **a** hip (Time had elapsed between their first shipment of stock and this new order.)

**16 d** starve

'Maintain' and (to a lesser extent) 'provide' and 'foster' have similar meanings, and 'taste' has a completely different meaning.

**17 b** unsure

'Definite' has a similar meaning, and 'reassure', 'assure' and 'ensure' have different meanings, although they are all related to certainty.

**18 a** expert

'Learner' has a similar meaning, and 'fresh', 'cold' and 'perforate' all have completely different meanings.

**19 e** few

'Many' has a similar meaning, and 'money', 'digits' and 'grew' all have different meanings.

**20 c** impossible

'Feasible' means 'doable' and 'possible'. 'Impossible' has the opposite meaning.

# Test 14

**1 b** proud

'Ashamed' has a similar meaning to 'embarrassed', and 'nervous', 'annoyed' and 'amazed' have completely different meanings.

**2 d** redundant

'Vital' and 'essential' both have similar meanings to 'necessary', and 'wanted' and 'irregular' have completely different meanings.

**3 a** unbiased

'Biased' has a similar meaning to 'prejudiced', and 'misinformed' and 'mistaken' have completely different meanings.

**4 d** unfamiliar

'Identified', 'knew', and (to a lesser extent) 'learnt' all have similar meanings to 'recognised', and 'suspicious' has a different meaning.

**5 b** unkempt

'Neat' can mean the same as 'tidy'. 'Unkempt' means the same as 'untidy'.

**6** eat (We should always blow out candles when we leave a room.)

**7** fog (The dark sky looked as though a storm was due OR The sky looked dark, as though a storm was due.)

**8** taken (We took the dog for a walk in the park.)

**9** country (In school, we are studying the Second World War OR We are studying the Second World War in school.)

10  have (Our family has had many memorable holidays in Wales OR variations such as: In Wales, our family has had many memorable holidays.)
11  **e**  r c i s (practise)
    **d** would give the noun form, but 'rehearse' is a verb so the verb form of 'practise' is required.
12  **d**  h l l d (chilled)
13  **b**  e d m (seldom)
14  **c**  o p e e s o (comprehension)
15  **a**  n i i i a t (insignificant)
16  The artist opened the **drawer** and took out her brushes, paint and mixing **palette**.
    'Drawer' describes part of a piece of furniture. A 'palette' is the board an artist uses to mix paint.
17  We need to be **discreet** if we are to move **forward** with the surprise party plans.
    'Discreet' can mean 'tactful' or 'subtle'. 'Forward' is an adjective meaning 'onwards'.
18  We experienced thunder and **lightning** before the rain began to **pour**.
    'Lightning' is a flash of bright light produced by electrical discharge. 'Pour' can mean 'flow' and, in the case of rain, 'fall heavily'.
19  He **passed** her a sweet as they stood patiently in the long **queue** at the cinema.
    'Passed' is the past tense of the verb 'to pass'. 'Queue' means 'a line of people'.
20  I made a list of names that **was** too long, so I needed to reduce **it** to a more manageable number.
    Although 'names' is plural, the reference is to 'list' (singular).

# Test 15

1  tem (excitement, temptation)
2  ern (government, southerners)
3  squ (grotesque, squeezing)
4  ita (inhabitants, digital)
5  elv (ourselves, shelving)
6  **b** (The official gave **advice to** the whole department.)
   Here, you need the noun 'advice', not the verb 'advise'. The preposition 'to' refers to the verb 'gave'.
7  **c** (Her eyes scanned the supermarket **aisle as** she looked for coconut milk.)
   An 'aisle' is a passage between shelves or seats. The word 'as' tells us when she scanned the aisle.
8  **c** (With **bated breath**, we watched in amazement at the scene.)
   'With bated breath' means 'very anxiously'. 'Baited' means 'annoyed' or 'tormented'.
9  **d** (Did the tree's **bough break** during the storm or was it cut on purpose?)
   A 'bough' is a branch of a tree, and 'break' is a verb meaning 'to split into pieces'.
10 **d** (We **sailed between** the two arches that spanned the river.)
   The sentence uses the past tense verb 'spanned', so 'sail' and 'sailing' are incorrect. The word 'between' refers to two items (two arches), while 'among' usually refers to more than two items.
11 **a**  relief
   'Relief' and 'release' can both be nouns meaning 'alleviation from pain or distress', or from a restriction of some kind. The other options are all verbs with different meanings.
12 **c**  insignificant
13 **b**  affliction
14 **e**  snatch
   'Shove' and 'push' both have opposite meanings. 'Large' and 'smaller' have completely different meanings.
15 **b**  spot
16 **c**  shrink
   'Increase' and 'lengthen' have similar meanings, and 'estate' and 'stress' have completely different meanings.
17 **b**  above
   'Under' and 'beneath' have similar meanings, and 'between' and 'with' have different meanings.
18 **c**  remember
   You can 'restore' something that has been forgotten or 'regain' a memory, but one of the meanings of 'remember' is 'not forget'.

**19  a**  permanent

'Flippant' and 'indifferent' have similar meanings, and 'for' and 'think' have completely different meanings.

**20  d**  timid

'Bold' can mean 'daring' and 'fearless'. 'Timid' means 'unadventurous' and 'afraid'.

## Test 16

**1  c**  playful

'Tricky' is similar because it can mean 'cunning' (as well as 'difficult'), but 'cunning' implies deceit, while 'playful' and 'mischievous' both imply good-natured mischief.

**2  b**  group

**3  a**  escort

'Accompany' and 'escort' are both verbs meaning 'to go with'. The other options are all nouns with other meanings.

**4  b**  debate

**5  d**  ravine

One of the meanings of 'gorge' is a 'deep valley'. 'Ravine' also means a 'deep valley'.

**6  a**  rain, **e**  hot

'Wind', 'rotate' and 'turn' all describe movement.

**7  b**  unjust, **d**  heavy

'Fair', 'pale' and 'light' can all be used to describe something with a soft or pastel colour.

**8  d**  innocent, **e**  unblemished

'Revenge', 'retaliation' and 'retribution' all mean 'reprisal'.

**9  a**  found, **c**  head

'Fund', 'back' and 'sponsor' all mean 'financially support'.

**10  b**  pence, **e**  sense

The words 'pound', 'pummel' and 'thump' can all mean 'to punch' or 'to beat'.

**11  e**  (After the funeral, family and friends left flowers at the **cemetery**.)

'Cemetery' means 'graveyard'.

**12  a**  (At the village hall, there was a meeting about local **concerns**.)

'Concerns' means 'interests' or 'worries'.

**13  d**  (The film was shown on the largest cinema **screen**.)

'Screen' is the best choice here.

**14  b**  (Isaac can't run in the race as he has pulled a **muscle** in his leg.)

'Muscle' is the best choice here because Isaac could only have pulled a muscle. A 'mussel' is a type of mollusc.

**15  e**  swam (The man stood on the cliff edge looking out to sea OR The man on the cliff edge stood looking out to sea.)

**16  a**  because (The car stopped at the lights, waiting for them to turn green.)

**17  b**  closed (I opened my present and was so excited to get the book.)

**18  e**  winter (It was so cold we put on our gloves, hat and scarf to keep warm. NB: 'gloves', 'hat' and 'scarf' can be given in any order.)

## Test 17

**1  a**  spoil, **o**  damage

If you 'ruin' something, you 'spoil' or 'damage' it.

**2  n**  residence, **r**  abode

Both mean 'the place where someone lives'.

**3  e**  basic, **t**  uncomplicated

'Basic' and 'uncomplicated' mean 'simple'.

**4  g**  dishevelled, **p**  untidy

Both 'dishevelled' and 'untidy' mean 'disordered'.

**5**  angrily (You must never look directly at the sun.)

**6**  kaleidoscope (A microscope makes small things appear bigger.)

**7**  chips (Jam on toast is my favourite breakfast OR My favourite breakfast is jam on toast.)

**8**  of (Our cat has had six fluffy kittens OR Our cat, Fluffy, has had six kittens.)

**9  a**  work

'Hobby', 'sport' and 'rest' are all types of 'leisure', so have a similar meaning, and 'test' has a completely different meaning.

**10  d**  professional

'Amateur' means 'not professional'.

**11  c**  separated.

'Attached' means 'connected to' and 'separated' means 'disconnected from'.

**12  b** praise

'Practise' has a similar meaning to 'mock' (in the sense of a 'mock exam') and 'pretend', 'precise' and 'preview' all have completely different meanings.

**13  a** imp (We caught a glimpse of the sea through the trees.)

**14  d** cat (School-trip places are allocated on a strictly first come, first served basis.)

**15  b** rug (We were struggling to get our suitcases into the taxi.)

**16  e** car (That was definitely the scariest story I have ever read!)

## Test 18

**1  a** car, **d** pea (He always carried a mirror to check his appearance.)

**2  b** tin, **d** her (The animal was hunted to extinction by poachers.)

**3  b** ice, **c** law (The priceless ring contained a flawless diamond.)

**4  d** gum, **e** due (After their argument, the two boys were now subdued.)

**5  c** donate

**6  b** collect

'Collect' is a synonym for 'raise' when talking about money.

**7  a** protests

Both 'protests' (noun) and 'objections' can mean 'statements of dissent or disapproval'.

**8  d** stopping

'Halting' progress means 'stopping' progress, but perhaps temporarily.

**9** thankful

**10** intention

**11** hazardous

**12** restore

**13  a** bright, **e** loud

'Quiet', 'noiseless' and 'hushed' can all mean 'peaceful'.

**14  b** straightening, **d** flexing

'Winding', 'curling' and 'spiralling' can all mean 'coiling'.

**15  d** fluffy, **e** cosy

'Stern', 'severe' and 'strict' can all mean 'harsh'.

**16  b** roughly, **c** approximately

'Dainty', 'graceful' and 'charming' can all be used to describe something that is delicate or pleasant.

## Test 19

**1** inconspicuous

**2** gregarious

**3** unorthodox

**4** unfathomable

**5  b** tally

You can keep a 'tally' or 'score' of the number of points awarded during a game, for example.

**6  e** unstable

'Steady' and 'calm' have opposite meanings, and 'core' and 'trill' have completely different meanings.

**7  c** gain

'Yield' and 'give' have opposite meanings, and 'wriggle' and 'scatter' have completely different meanings.

**8  a** weakened

'Strong' and 'enriched' have opposite meanings, and 'cheap' and 'expensive' have completely different meanings.

**9  e** assess

'Assess' means 'to judge' or 'weigh up' and 'evaluate' means the same as 'assess'.

**10  d** botch

Both 'bungle' and 'botch' mean 'to make a big mistake'.

**11  c** (She was asked to **practise chords** for her next keyboard lesson.)

'Practise' and 'practice' follow the same rule as 'advise' and 'advice' – 's' for the verb and 'c' for the noun. 'Chords' are groups of musical notes sounded together.

**12  a** (The **fourth storey** apartment overlooked both the park and river.)

'Fourth' relates to the number 'four' and 'storey' means one floor of a building.

**13 c** (He tried to **pour cereal** into the bowl, but spilt it over the table top.)

'Pour' means 'to tip', and 'cereal' is edible grain.

**14 b** (You must **ensure draught** excluders are placed next to doors.)

'Ensure' means 'to make sure', and 'draught' means 'a current of air'.

**15 b** down (I was so fed up when I broke my leg playing hockey OR When I broke my leg playing hockey, I was so fed up.)

**16 c** grandmother (My little brother is going to his first party on Saturday OR On Saturday, my little brother is going to his first party.)

**17 b** custard (If I can choose, I prefer mushroom and pineapple on my pizza OR I prefer mushroom and pineapple on my pizza, if I can choose.)

**18 e** tree (I love to walk the dog in our local park OR I love to walk our dog in the local park.)

## Test 20

**1 d** u r c s (purchaser)

'Purchaser' means 'someone who buys something'.

**2 d** o e g (foreign)

'Foreign' can mean 'from elsewhere'.

**3 c** o u e (focused)

'Focused' can mean 'concentrated' or 'undistracted'.

**4 e** o c a e (concealed)

'Concealed' can mean 'hidden'.

**5 a** redress

'Unfairness' has an opposite meaning to 'justice', and 'undress', 'coldness' and 'partial' all have completely different meanings.

**6 c** ban

'Permit' has an opposite meaning to 'forbid', and 'badge', 'banner' and 'scary' all have completely different meanings.

**7 c** sunken

'Solid', 'sincere' and (to a lesser extent) 'substantial' have opposite meanings to 'hollow', and 'siding' has a completely different meaning.

**8 a** odorous

'Odorous' means 'having a scent' and can be used to describe both pleasant and unpleasant smells, while 'stinking' and 'noxious' are only used to describe unpleasant smells.

**9 d** attack

One of the meanings of 'charge' is 'to attack'.

**10 b** sell

'Peddle' means 'to trade' or 'to sell'.

**11 b** persuade, **h** convince

If you 'coax' someone, you try to 'persuade' or 'convince' them.

**12 j** cordial, **s** friendly

A 'companionable' person is 'friendly' or 'cordial'.

**13 k** narrow, **q** slender

Both 'narrow' and 'slender' mean 'lacking breadth'.

**14 d** advance, **t** progress

Both 'advance' and 'progress' mean 'to go forward'.

**15** bre (abbreviate, breakfast)

**16** rge (gorgeous, detergents)

**17** wle (flawless, knowledge)

**18** cei (deceitful, ceiling)

**19** nda (secondary, bandages)

**20** ash (dishwasher, fashionable)

## Test 21

**1** abi (habitable, capability)

**2** ngu (language, distinguish)

**3** iam (parliament, diameter)

**4** erc (handkerchief, commercial)

**5** mit (permitted, primitive)

**6 a** (The tired team drank orange juice to **quench** their thirst.)

'Quench' means 'satisfy' and suggests the use of liquid.

**7 d** (The **stout** man placed a fleshy finger against his chubby lips.)

'Stout' means 'plump', and a man with fleshy fingers and chubby lips is likely to be plump.

8 **c** (In the **twilight**, the tired miner returned home after an exhausting day.)

'Twilight' means 'dusk' or 'nightfall'. 'After an exhausting day' implies it is evening.

9 **b** (A red sky at night is a favourable **omen** of nice weather.)

'Omen' means 'sign'.

10 **b** (As the rain stopped, the freshly scented roses **perfumed** the summer evening.)

'Perfumed' means the same as 'scented'.

11 **a** combination, **q** merger

Both describe the coming together of two or more things.

12 **f** apprehensive, **l** worried

An 'anxious' person is 'apprehensive' and 'worried'.

13 **j** vigorous, **t** robust

Both 'robust' and 'vigorous' mean 'strong'.

14 **d** productive, **n** fertile

Both 'fertile' and 'productive' can mean 'fruitful'.

15 **c** dutiful

'Unruly' and 'naughty' have opposite meanings, and 'restless' and 'rewarding' have completely different meanings.

16 **d** positive

17 **a** specific

18 **b** cleanse

'Cleanse' is a better choice than 'clear' because 'purify' and 'cleanse' are both verbs that can mean 'make pure', while 'clear' as a verb can mean 'make free of something' but does not on its own imply purity.

## Test 22

1 **a** restricted

'Restricted' is a better choice than 'lack' because 'restricted' and 'ample' can both be used as adjectives, as in 'ample choice' and 'restricted choice', while 'lack' cannot.

2 **d** debit

'Honour' and 'tribute' both have similar meanings to 'credit', while 'cards' and 'account' have completely different meanings.

3 **b** gather

'Scatter' and 'spray' both have similar meanings to 'disperse'. 'Dissolve' means 'to break up' and 'dislodge' means 'to knock loose'.

4 **a** delicious

'Rotten' and 'unsavoury' both have similar meanings to 'inedible', which means 'not fit for eating'. 'Tired' and 'well' have completely different meanings.

5 perceives

6 remorse

7 revered

8 prank

9 wealth (She could not influence the opinion of the judges.)

10 swans (The dog bounded into the sea chasing an imaginary ball OR The dog, chasing an imaginary ball, bounded into the sea OR Chasing an imaginary ball, the dog bounded into the sea.)

11 pencil (He drew the curtains and switched on the light OR He switched on the light and drew the curtains.)

12 drink (She felt sick and regretted eating her meal so quickly.)

13–16 **(13)** enough: means 'to the required degree'.

**(14)** across: describes where the seat belt is. It is a better choice than 'on' because 'across' tells us the seat belt went from one side to the other, whereas 'on' would imply the item on his lap was not attached to anything.

**(15)** then: indicates that we are going to be told what happened next, after Rami was lifted higher and higher.

**(16)** with: 'with a mixture of fear and pleasure' describes how Rami squealed.

## Test 23

1 **e** cut

None of the other options have meanings similar to 'incision', although an incisor is a type of tooth.

2 **b** talk

None of the other options have meanings similar to 'address'. We 'live' at an 'address', but the meanings of these two words are not similar.

3  **a** embellishment

A 'ribbon' is a type of decoration, but does not mean 'decoration'.

4  **c** spray

'Spray' means 'a fine burst of water', but it also means 'a sprig of flowers or leaves'. A 'sprig' is a small branch or shoot of a plant.

5  **b** stimulated
6  **a** vegetation
7  **b** costs
8  **a** submitted

If an employee has 'deposited' her expenses with the accounts office, she has submitted them so they can be paid.

9  welcome
10  inaudible
11  pompous
12  prosperous
13  rio (curiously, luxurious)
14  ess (aggressive, essentials)
15  ast (devastated, coastline)
16  urs (excursion, neighbours)

## Test 24

1  aur (restaurant, thesaurus)
2  lar (polarity, burglaries)
3  imu (minimum, simulator)
4  nta (intangible, accidental)
5  **a** race, **d** jump

'Pace', 'step' and 'stride' are all words to do with walking.

6  **d** medal, **e** ribbon

'Defend', 'protect' and 'shield' all mean 'to cushion' or 'to keep safe'.

7  **a** trivial, **b** insignificant

'Central', 'crucial' and 'fundamental' all mean 'very important'.

8  **a** expose, **e** reveal

'Dodge', 'evade' and 'avoid' can all mean 'to escape'.

9  **e** imprecise

10  **a** resistant

'Obedient' has a similar meaning to 'submissive', and 'weak', 'understanding' and 'underused' have completely different meanings.

11  **c** small

'Massive' has a similar meaning to 'vast', and 'vain', 'septic' and 'cast' have completely different meanings.

12  **d** ineffective
13  **c** natural

The word 'pretentious' can mean 'ornate'. The word 'natural' can mean 'plain' and 'simple'.

14  **e** winter (On the fifth of November we celebrate Bonfire Night OR We celebrate Bonfire Night on the fifth of November.)

15  **d** lamb (A little hedgehog is hibernating in our garden this year OR This year, a little hedgehog is hibernating in our garden OR A hedgehog is hibernating in our little garden this year OR This year, a hedgehog is hibernating in our little garden.)

16  **c** of (There are adverts between programmes on some television channels OR On some television channels, there are adverts between programmes OR There are adverts between television programmes on some channels OR On some channels, there are adverts between television programmes.)

17  **e** carton (I put some raspberry sauce on my fruit and ice cream OR I put some sauce on my fruit and raspberry ice cream.)

18  **c** house (She spent hours getting rid of the weeds in the garden OR She spent hours in the garden getting rid of the weeds.)

## Test 25

1  **b** and, **e** lie (After her accident, the bandage was applied to the wound.)

2  **e** elf, **c** cat (It was her twelfth day on medication and she felt a little better.)

3  **d** lug, **a** bud (We couldn't take much luggage on the budget airline.)

4  **d** err, **b** ran (The holly berries were enjoyed by a range of birds.)

5  **a** car, **e** rot (The fields had jaunty scarecrows protecting the newly sown seed.)

6  **c**  absolute
7  **a**  sign
8  **b**  ease

'Difficulty' has an opposite meaning, and the other three options have completely different meanings.

9  **a**  exhaustive

'Slapdash' has an opposite meaning, and none of the other options have meanings similar to 'thorough'.

10  **e**  toddle

The words 'waddle' and 'toddle' can both mean 'to totter' or 'to walk unsteadily', as a child just learning to walk might.

11  **a**  (The games designers were trying to **develop** a new and exciting app.)

'Develop' means 'to create', and developing apps is what games designers do.

12  **c**  (The **thermometer** recorded the temperature on a regular basis.)

Thermometers measure temperature.

13  **a**  (The teacher **appreciated** how much work the choir had done, as their singing was superb.)

'Appreciated' means 'recognised' and indicates a positive opinion. We know it must be positive because the 'singing was superb'.

14  **b**  (The two little boys tried to **communicate** with walkie-talkie radios.)

'Communicate' means 'to exchange ideas and opinions' and implies both speaking and listening.

15  **d**  pinch, **e**  speck

'Chunk', 'lump' and 'slab' all mean a 'block' of something.

16  **c**  tasty, **d**  flavoursome

'Aromatic', 'fragrant' and 'perfumed' all mean 'scented'.

17  **a**  slug, **b**  worm

All the words are creatures, but 'lizard', 'tortoise' and 'crocodile' are all reptiles.

18  **a**  star, **e**  moon

'Twinkle', 'glisten' and 'glitter' can all mean 'sparkle'.

# Test 26

1  **a**  fatigue, **t**  lethargy

Both describe a state of tiredness.

2  **h**  smooth, **l**  shiny

A cat with a 'sleek' coat has 'shiny', 'smooth' fur.

3  **o**  quarrel, **p**  dispute

Both 'dispute' and 'quarrel' mean 'to disagree'.

4  **e**  amicable, **r**  friendly

Both 'friendly' and 'amicable' can mean 'kind' or 'well-meaning'.

5  **b**  banned

'Banned' and 'prohibited' mean 'not allowed'.

6  **d**  residents

'Residents' and 'inhabitants' can both be used to describe the people who live somewhere.

7  **c**  surrounded

'Besieged' can be used to describe a place that is under attack in some way by someone or something, or is 'surrounded' by difficulty.

8  **a**  deaths

'Fatalities' are deaths caused by accident, natural disaster, war, and so on.

9  **e**  sum (He had already consumed four bananas and a chocolate bar.)

10  **b**  lap (The vacant house was so run-down and dilapidated.)

11  **c**  arm (The garment was embroidered with gold and silver thread.)

12  **e**  lad (Marmalade was easily made alongside other conserves.)

13  **e**  rubbish

'Rubbish' and 'refuse' both mean 'waste'.

14  **a**  dependable

'Dishonest' and (to a lesser extent) 'dreadful' and 'false' have opposite meanings, and 'decline' has a completely different meaning.

15  **d**  pushed

'Nudged' is a close option, but not as aggressive as 'pushed' or 'shoved'.

16  **a**  burn

## Test 27

1. **a** ethereal

   'Real' and 'obvious' have opposite meanings, and 'tangy' and 'unappetising' have completely different meanings.

2. **d** freedom

   'Lightness' has a similar meaning in that it suggests no restraints, but its meaning doesn't cover 'autonomy' or 'free will' as 'freedom' and 'liberty' do.

3. **e** persecute

4. **b** trickster

   'Comedian' and 'clown' are similar, but 'trickster' and 'rogue' both imply cunning or deceit, which 'comedian' and 'clown' do not.

5. **c** inconvenience

   The word 'bother' can mean 'trouble' or 'hassle'. The word 'inconvenience' can have the same meaning.

6. **a** congeal

   The word 'congeal' means 'to set' or 'to thicken'. The word 'clot' can mean the same.

7. loyalist

8. compressed

9. unprotected

10. lethargic

11. **d** (If anyone trips over the cable, we are **liable**, so make it safe.)

    'Liable' means 'legally responsible'.

12. **a** (Breathe in quickly, then **exhale** slowly to get rid of nervousness.)

    'Exhale' means 'to breathe out'.

13. **d** (The glass was blown and the window frame **charred** from the fire.)

    'Charred' means 'scorched' or 'burnt'.

14. **b** (If you **harass** the dog it makes her angry and she might bite you.)

    'Harass' means 'to annoy' or 'to tease'.

15. **d** shoes (Her new red shorts had two pockets and a belt OR Her new shorts had two pockets and a red belt OR Her new shorts had two red pockets and a belt.)

16. **e** the (The brightly painted poster was stuck firmly on the door OR The poster was stuck firmly on the brightly painted door.)

17. **c** high (The vase was full of beautifully scented flowers.)

18. **c** soil (The dog ran down the garden with a huge, juicy bone OR The huge dog ran down the garden with a juicy bone.)

## Test 28

1. **c** pan (We would love you to accompany us to the party.)

2. **e** now (The teacher acknowledged the children's hard work.)

3. **c** err (Please do not interrupt me when I am talking.)

4. **d** one (The scientist was a pioneer in genetic research.)

5. **c** (Chrissy loved to **sail a dinghy** on the River Dee.)

   'Sail' is a verb meaning 'to travel in a boat' and a 'dinghy' is a type of small boat.

6. **d** (He was so **nosy he wondered** what was in the locked drawer.)

   'Nosy' means 'curious' or 'prying', and 'wondered' means 'speculated' or 'wanted to know'.

7. **b** (The lion crouched low so he could **stare at his prey** before pouncing.)

   'Stare' is a verb meaning 'to look intently' and 'prey' is a noun meaning 'hunted animal'.

8. **d** (The **convoy was covert** as it undertook an undercover operation.)

   'Convoy' is a collective noun requiring a singular verb, and 'covert' is an adjective meaning 'secretive'.

9. **c** mild

   'Feral' and 'wild' both have similar meanings to 'brutish', and 'bruised' and 'feline' have completely different meanings.

10. **a** elated

    'Gloomy' has a similar meaning to 'despondent', and 'detailed', 'gloating' and 'write' have completely different meanings.

**11 b** obscure

'Clear', 'understandable' and (to a lesser extent) 'light' all have similar meanings to 'lucid', and 'weighty' has a completely different meaning.

**12 e** separate

'Amalgamate', 'merge' and 'fuse' all have similar meanings to 'meld', and 'twist' has a completely different meaning.

**13 c** recede

'Advance' can mean 'to move forward'. 'Recede' can mean 'to move backwards'.

**14 d** rejoice

'Grieve' means 'to mourn' or 'to cry'. 'Rejoice' can mean 'to celebrate'.

**15 c** basic, **e** threadbare

'Opulent', 'palatial' and 'sumptuous' can all be used to describe something that is luxurious.

**16 a** insubstantial, **b** fragile

'Hefty', 'weighty' and 'solid' can all be used to mean 'heavy'.

**17 c** charcoal, **d** grey

All the words are colours but 'lilac', 'lavender' and 'violet' are shades of purple, and they are all plants.

**18 a** sleep, **d** snore

'Drift', 'sail' and 'glide' can all be used to describe something that floats.

**19 b** cupped, **d** outside

'Template', 'outline' and 'specification' can all mean 'pattern' or 'mould'.

**20 a** tiptoe, **b** patter

'Bawl', 'howl' and 'bellow' can all mean 'to cry' or 'to screech'.

# Test 29

**1 c** e a c o y (melancholy)

'Melancholy' means 'sadness'.

**2 a** i i t r (miniature)

'Miniature' means 'very small'.

**3 e** p p i t i (opposition)

'Opposition' means 'resistance' or 'disagreement'.

**4 c** e u s v (repulsive)

'Repulsive' means 'disgusting'.

**5 b** t i t e (intricate)

'Intricate' means 'complex' or 'complicated'.

**6 c** flustered

'Placid' and 'calm' have opposite meanings, and 'mature' and 'sad' have completely different meanings.

**7 b** obvious

'Unclear' has an opposite meaning, and the other three options have completely different meanings.

**8 d** penitent

**9 c** pale

'Flushed', 'bright' and 'dark' have opposite meanings, and 'majestic' has a completely different meaning.

**10 e** energy

'Spirit' can mean 'enthusiasm' and 'drive'. The word 'energy' can mean the same.

**11 c** whole, **d** entire

'Partial', 'section' and 'fragment' can all be used to describe part of something.

**12 b** starve, **d** kill

'Nourish', 'nurture' and 'encourage' all mean 'to sustain' or 'to support'.

**13 a** goods, **b** sell

'Buy', 'acquire' and 'purchase' are all ways of obtaining something.

**14 d** taut, **e** tense

'Nimble', 'supple' and 'agile' can be used to describe quick, light or flexible movement.

**15 b** contain, **d** long

'Condensed', 'short' and 'brief' all describe something that is said or written in a few words.

**16 c** motivate

**17 a** easily

'Hardly' has a similar meaning to 'barely', and 'softly,' 'roughly' and 'gently' all have completely different meanings.

**18 d** punish

'Forgive' and 'apologise' both have similar meanings, and 'warrant' and 'trial' have completely different meanings.

**19  d** active

'Sleepy', 'sluggish' and 'immobile' could all be used to describe something that is 'dormant', and 'rare' has a completely different meaning.

**20  c** adore

'Detest' is a synonym for 'despise', while 'snub', 'disgust' and 'defy' have completely different meanings.

## Test 30

**1  c** optimistic

**2  d** base

'Culminate' and 'summit' both have similar meanings to 'pinnacle'.

**3  b** expand

'Contract' has a similar meaning to 'abbreviate'.

**4  c** lofty

'Common' and (to a lesser extent) 'average' and 'inferior' have similar meanings to 'lowly'.

**5  a** obstruct

'Encourage' can mean 'to help' or 'to promote'. 'Obstruct' can mean 'to stop', 'to block' or 'to prevent'.

**6  e** unique

'Ordinary' means 'plain' and 'common'. 'Unique' means 'individual' and 'rare'.

**7** wider (The days were getting shorter and the nights longer OR The days were getting longer and the nights shorter OR The nights were getting shorter and the days longer OR The nights were getting longer and the days shorter.)

**8** sky (The autumn leaves had fallen to the ground.)

**9** grass (There were lots of brown conkers under the tree.)

**10** were (There was the smell of bonfires in the air OR The smell of bonfires was there in the air.)

**11** garden (Some monkeys spend all day protecting their home in the forest.)

**12** diamond (There are seven distinct colours of the rainbow.)

**13  c** n i t (anxiety)

**14  e** e o m n (recommend)

**15  b** o p e (complex)

**16  a** n e r p (interrupt)

**17  d** s o d g (astounding)

**18  c** (The ship had been torpedoed during the war.)

**19  b** (The author had a real skill in describing his characters.)

**20  a** (I had to introduce the school choir at our end of term concert.)

**21  e** (He kept stubbing his toe on the radiator.)

# PUZZLE ANSWERS

## Puzzle 1

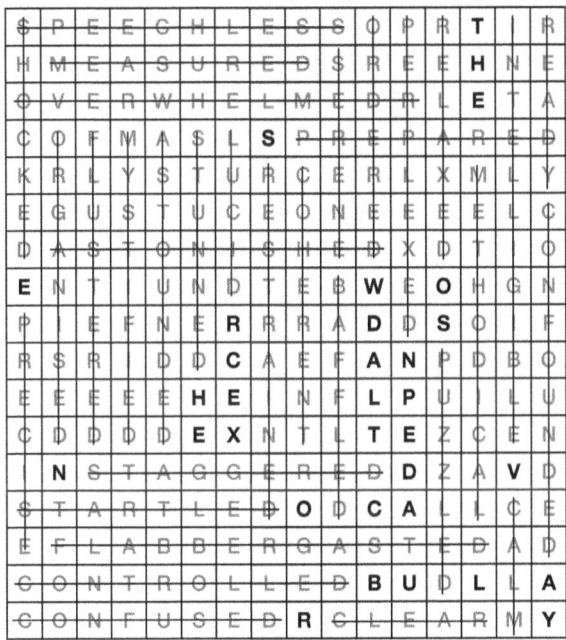

Sixteen of the adjectives describe someone who is confused or surprised (astonished, confused, overwhelmed, speechless, astounded, flabbergasted, perplexed, startled, baffled, flustered, puzzled, stunned, confounded, mystified, shocked, staggered). The others describe someone or something that is calm and ordered (calm, intelligible, ordered, ready, clear, lucid, organised, relaxed, coherent, measured, precise, restrained, controlled, methodical, prepared, serene).

**Hidden message:** THESE WORDS CAN HELP EXTEND VOCABULARY.

## Puzzle 2

**Birds:** robin, starling, blackbird, pigeon, eagle, owl, magpie, blue tit. **Trees:** oak, pine, sycamore, rowan, hawthorn, maple, birch, fir. **Flowers:** rose, lily, tulip, daffodil, iris, bluebell, daisy, poppy. **Metals:** gold, silver, iron, zinc, aluminium, tin, bronze, copper.

## Puzzle 3

There is more than one way to fill in the grid correctly. This is one of them. (Note that WEAK is the only four-letter word, so begin by filling that in as your starting point.)

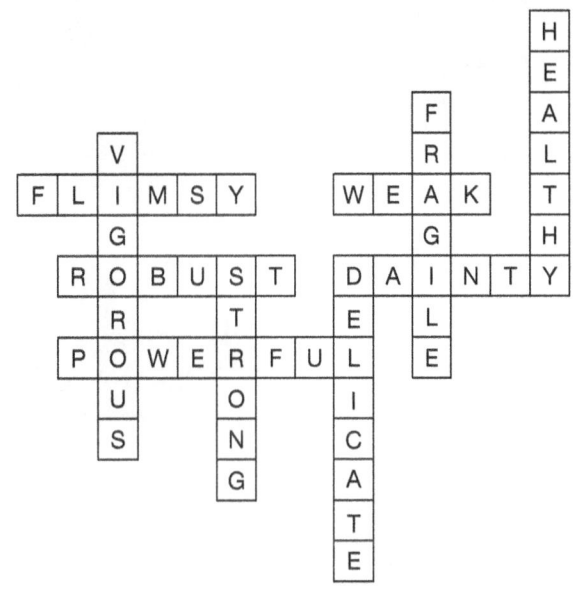

## Puzzle 4

Here are some suggested answers, but other answers that start with the correct letter are also acceptable. Check that your answers all match the categories.

**C:** Clair, cook, carefully, cat, cake, careful

**D:** Divya, dancer, delicately, dog, dumplings, difficult

**F:** Finn, farmer, fairly, fox, fish, friendly

**G:** George, gardener, gaudily, giraffe, grapes, great

**H:** Helen, hairdresser, happily, horse, ham, horrible

**L:** Li, lawyer, leniently, lion, lasagne, long

**M:** Matthew, mechanic, majestically, monkey, milk, mild

**N:** Noah, nurse, neatly, newt, noodles, nasty

## Puzzle 5

Hint: CUT is the only three-letter word, NEAT is the only four-letter word, and CULTIVATED is the only ten-letter word, so begin by filling those in as your starting point.

## Puzzle 9

In some cases, various homophones are possible. Here are some examples:

bawled, bald; bury, berry; due, dew; bawl, ball; discreet, discrete; days, daze; carrot, carat; brooch, broach; oar, ore, or; cash, cache; throne, thrown; bow, bough; bard, barred; board, bored; boy, buoy; pray, prey; minor, miner; birth, berth; baron, barren; sole, soul; air, heir; principal, principle; bread, bred; draft, draught; dough, doe; dual, duel; censor, sensor; maze, maize; mall, maul; manner, manor; medal, meddle; taught, taut; bite, byte; sachet, sashay; sear, seer; serf, surf; sheer, shear; slay, sleigh; naval, navel; steak, stake; sweet, suite; nay, neigh; cymbal, symbol; paws, pause; wail, whale; pedal, peddle; Sunday, sundae; wave, waive

## Puzzle 6

Here are some suggested answers, but other answers that work are also acceptable:

**Fish:** cod, plaice, eel, tuna, trout
**Birds:** owl, swift, eagle, crow, tern
**Insects:** ant, fly, bee, wasp, louse
**Mammals:** cat, goat, bear, rat, sheep

## Puzzle 7

maximum, minimum; transparent, opaque; virtue, vice; optimist, pessimist; feral, domesticated; joy, sorrow; permanent, temporary; mandatory, optional; grave, trivial; complicated, simple; spacious, restricted; object, approve; negligent, careful; calm, turbulent; authentic, fake; boastful, humble; pacify, inflame

For some words, more than one pair is possible. For example, 'calm' (verb) is an antonym of 'inflame'. However, 'turbulent' can only be paired with 'calm' (adjective), and 'pacify' can only be paired with 'inflame'.

## Puzzle 8

**Chain 1:** great, thriving, gorgeous, secure, evil, light, terrific, cheer, repellent, terrible
Only one word in the list can go in each of boxes 3 to 6. The sixth word ends in T, so the seventh must be TERRIFIC or TERRIBLE. There is no word left beginning with E, so the seventh word must be TERRIFIC and the eighth CHEER.

**Chain 2:** dying, genuine, excellent, thrilling, grim, mean, nastiness, sad, decaying, grief OR decaying, genuine, excellent, thrilling, grim, mean, nastiness, sad, dying, grief

## Puzzle 10

**List 1:** whole, total (The other words are all synonyms for the word 'part'.)
**List 2:** domed, shade (The other words are all synonyms for 'outer'.)
**List 3:** cuddled, curved (The other words all describe food that has gone bad.)
**List 4:** arched, rounded (The other words are synonyms for 'sharp'.)
**List 5:** tint, hue (The other words all describe dismal weather.)
**List 6:** full, complete (The other words are all measuring terms.)
**List 7:** hugged, tone (The other words all mean to help someone.)
**List 8:** embraced, held (The other words all mean to leave out or ignore.)
**Lists 9–12:** tone, hue, shade, tint (words connected to colour); whole, complete, full, total (synonyms for 'wholeness'); curved, arched, rounded, domed (words describing smooth surfaces); hugged, cuddled, embraced, held (synonyms for 'hugged')

## Puzzle 11

**1** rein, rain, reign; French, Italian, German; boiled, roasted, fried; wind, turn, twist; lubricate, oil, grease
**2** ferocious, brutal, vicious; gaudy, garish, lurid; honest, truthful, candid; expressive, animated, communicative; cautious, wary, vigilant
**3** eyelash, eyelid, eyeball; bluebell, blueprint, blueberry; seafood, seaweed, seaside; snowman, snowdrop, snowflake; footplate, footpath, footstep

# Test 18 continued from page 38

Complete the word on the right so that it has the **SAME** or **SIMILAR** meaning to the word on the left.

9  grateful    | t | h |   |   |   |   |   | l |

10 purpose    | i | n |   |   |   | i | o | n |

11 perilous   | h | a | z |   |   |   |   | s |

12 revive     |   |   |   | t | o | r | e |

Select the **TWO** odd words out on each line. Select your answers by underlining **TWO** of the options **a–e**.

13  a bright     b quiet         c noiseless      d hushed      e loud

14  a winding    b straightening c curling        d flexing     e spiralling

15  a stern      b severe        c strict         d fluffy      e cosy

16  a dainty     b roughly       c approximately  d graceful    e charming

# Test 19

Complete the word on the right so that it has an **OPPOSITE** meaning to the word on the left.

1  obvious       i n c o n s _ _ _ _ _ _ (inconspicuous)

2  unsociable    g _ _ _ _ _ _ _ u s (gregarious)

3  conventional  u n o _ _ _ o d o _ (unorthodox)

4  shallow       u n f _ _ _ _ _ a b l e (unfathomable)

Select the **ONE** word on the right that has the most **SIMILAR** meaning to the word on the left. Underline the correct answer.

5  score     **a** scissors    **b** tally    **c** part    **d** partner    **e** take

6  volatile  **a** steady    **b** calm    **c** core    **d** trill    **e** unstable

7  acquire   **a** yield    **b** give    **c** gain    **d** wriggle    **e** scatter

8  diluted   **a** weakened    **b** strong    **c** cheap    **d** enriched    **e** expensive

9  evaluate  **a** remote    **b** convert    **c** invent    **d** incense    **e** assess

10 bungle    **a** mash    **b** tangle    **c** tingle    **d** botch    **e** batch

The following sentences all have a short phrase missing. Complete each sentence by underlining a phrase from options **a–d**.

11  She was asked to _____ for her next keyboard lesson.

   **a** practise cords   **b** practice cords   **c** practise chords   **d** practice chords

12  The _____ apartment overlooked both the park and river.

   **a** fourth storey   **b** forth story   **c** fourth story   **d** forth storey

13  He tried to _____ into the bowl, but spilt it over the table top.

   **a** pour serial   **b** pore serial   **c** pour cereal   **d** pore cereal

14  You must _____ excluders are placed next to doors.

   **a** insure draught   **b** ensure draught   **c** insure draft   **d** ensure draft

These sentences have been jumbled up and all have **ONE** extra word. Select the extra word in each of the sentences by underlining **ONE** word from options **a–e**.

15  hockey I down playing up was leg so my fed broke when I

   **a** broke   **b** down   **c** fed   **d** hockey   **e** playing

16  my is little grandmother going brother to Saturday party on first his

   **a** brother   **b** going   **c** grandmother   **d** little   **e** party

17  if pizza my I can on pineapple custard choose I and mushroom prefer

   **a** choose   **b** custard   **c** mushroom   **d** pizza   **e** prefer

18  the in walk tree our to local love park I dog

   **a** dog   **b** local   **c** love   **d** park   **e** tree

*Time for a break! ★ Go to Puzzle Page 90 →*

# Test 20

Find the missing letters that complete the word on the right so that it has an **OPPOSITE** meaning to the word on the left. Underline the correct answer from options **a–e**.

1  seller    p _ _ _ h a _ er
   **a** ersp   **b** artn   **c** arts   **d** urcs   **e** urtv

2  local    f _ r _ i _ n
   **a** ike   **b** oee   **c** ika   **d** oeg   **e** ura

3  distracted    f _ c _ s _ d
   **a** ohe   **b** ose   **c** oue   **d** oeu   **e** oae

4  revealed    c _ n _ e _ l _ d
   **a** atre   **b** etre   **c** inae   **d** osae   **e** ocae

Underline the **ONE** word on the right that has the most **SIMILAR** meaning to the word given.

5  justice    **a** redress   **b** undress   **c** unfairness   **d** coldness   **e** partial

6  forbid    **a** permit   **b** badge   **c** ban   **d** banner   **e** scary

7  hollow    **a** substantial   **b** solid   **c** sunken   **d** siding   **e** sincere

8  fragrant    **a** odorous   **b** stinking   **c** noxious   **d** bland   **e** tasteless

9  charge    **a** notes   **b** expensive   **c** absolve   **d** attack   **e** soothe

10  peddle    **a** brake   **b** sell   **c** resolve   **d** spin   **e** cycle

Look at the words in the grid and then use them to answer the questions that follow.

| a adopt | b persuade | c embrace | d advance | e relaxed |
|---|---|---|---|---|
| f suspend | g dictionary | h convince | i mare | j cordial |
| k narrow | l minor | m mayor | n mild | o belligerent |
| p comfortable | q slender | r candidate | s friendly | t progress |

11  Find **TWO SYNONYMS** for the word 'coax'.

_____    _____

12  Find **TWO SYNONYMS** for the word 'companionable'.

_____    _____

13  Find **TWO ANTONYMS** for the word 'broad'.

_____    _____

14  Find **TWO ANTONYMS** for the word 'retreat'.

_____    _____

Find the missing three letters that complete these words. The three letters do not have to make a word. The same three letters are used for both words.

15  ab_____viate        _____akfast

16  go_____ous          dete_____nts

17  fla_____ss          kno_____dge

18  de_____tful         _____ling

19  seco_____ry         ba_____ges

20  dishw_____er        f_____ionable

# Test 21

Find the missing three letters that complete these words. The three letters do not have to make a word. The same three letters are used for both words.

1  h_____table         cap_____lity

2  la_____age          disti_____ish

3  parl_____ent        d_____eter

4  handk_____hief      comm_____ial

5  per_____ted         pri_____ive

The following sentences all have **ONE** word missing. Complete each sentence by underlining a word from options **a–e**.

6  The tired team drank orange juice to _____ their thirst.
   **a** quench   **b** quail   **c** quest   **d** quick   **e** queue

7  The _____ man placed a fleshy finger against his chubby lips.
   **a** lean   **b** long   **c** knight   **d** stout   **e** scour

8  In the _____, the tired miner returned home after an exhausting day.
   **a** dawn   **b** noon   **c** twilight   **d** daybreak   **e** sunrise

9  A red sky at night is a favourable _____ of nice weather.
   **a** view   **b** omen   **c** season   **d** story   **e** hope

10  As the rain stopped, the freshly scented roses _____ the summer evening.
    **a** lit   **b** perfumed   **c** touched   **d** stunted   **e** lengthened

Look at the words in the grid and then use them to answer the questions that follow.

| a combination | b college | c collage | d productive | e absence |
| f apprehensive | g enterprise | h estimate | i deliberate | j vigorous |
| k business | l worried | m comrade | n fertile | o people |
| p famine | q merger | r arduous | s purple | t robust |

11  Find **TWO SYNONYMS** for the word 'union'.

    _____    _____

12  Find **TWO SYNONYMS** for the word 'anxious'.

    _____    _____

13  Find **TWO ANTONYMS** for the word 'feeble'.

    _____    _____

14  Find **TWO ANTONYMS** for the word 'barren'.

    _____    _____

*Vocabulary Grid Tip!*
Remember that some words have more than one meaning. As you look through the words in the grid, try to think how many meanings of the word there are.

---

Select the **ONE** word on the right that has the most **SIMILAR** meaning to the word on the left. Underline the correct answer.

15  obedient    a restless    b rewarding    c dutiful    d unruly    e naughty

16  optimistic  a removal     b satisfy      c ordinary   d positive  e pleased

17  particular  a specific    b spineless    c amenable   d process   e formed

18  purify      a quarry      b cleanse      c bleach     d clear     e muddy

# Test 22

Select the **ONE** word on the right that has the most **OPPOSITE** meaning to the word on the left. Underline the correct answer.

1  ample      a restricted    b extensive    c plenty       d example    e lack

2  credit     a honour        b tribute      c cards        d debit      e account

3  disperse   a dissolve      b gather       c dislodge     d scatter    e spray

4  inedible   a delicious     b rotten       c unsavoury    d tired      e well

Complete the word on the right so that it has the **SAME** or **SIMILAR** meaning to the word on the left.

5  senses      p _ r c _ i v _ s

6  repentance  r _ m _ r _ e

7  venerable   r e _ _ r e _

8  hoax       _ r _ n _

### Reading Tip!

Spellings, as well as word knowledge, are crucial for these questions. The best way to extend your vocabulary and spelling ability is to read a wide range of books, comics and magazines. You could even create your own spelling lists to learn, or make vocabulary flashcards.

These sentences have been jumbled up and all have **ONE** extra word. Underline the word that is not needed.

9   the wealth of judges not she could influence opinion the

10  ball imaginary an swans chasing sea the bounded the into dog

11  he pencil drew switched light curtains on the and the

12  quickly drink so felt regretted sick and she eating meal her

---

Read the following paragraph and add one word from the list to each space so that the paragraph makes sense. There are more words than there are spaces so some will be left out, but each word can only be used once.

| across | because | enough | for | on | then | therefore | with |

13–16  Rami was excited. He had never been tall _____ to go on the ride before, but now he had grown another three and a half centimetres. He climbed up the steps and sat down in his seat, fastening the seat belt _____ his lap. He was so excited! It only took a couple of minutes before the music started and the ride whirred into action. Rami was lifted higher and higher, _____ the ride plunged dramatically towards the water. He squealed _____ a mixture of fear and pleasure as the ride raced around the corner and up another steep climb to the highest point.

# Test 23

Underline the **ONE** word from options **a–e** that has the most **SIMILAR** meaning to the word given.

1  incision    **a** make    **b** anger    **c** teeth    **d** internal    **e** cut

2  address     **a** live    **b** talk    **c** cry    **d** feint    **e** number

3  decoration  **a** embellishment    **b** stir    **c** cleanse    **d** ribbon    **e** clear

4  sprig       **a** jumpy    **b** shy    **c** spray    **d** custom    **e** fake

Read the following sentences and answer the questions. Underline the most sensible word from options **a–d**.

'The artist was inspired by the flora of nature.'

5  What does the word 'inspired' mean in this sentence?

   **a** simulated    **b** stimulated    **c** spiralled    **d** renovated

6  What does the word 'flora' mean in this sentence?

   **a** vegetation    **b** variation    **c** variegated    **d** renovated

'All expenses must be deposited with the accounts office.'

7  What does the word 'expenses' mean in this sentence?

   **a** dear    **b** costs    **c** cheap    **d** incomes

8  What does the word 'deposited' mean in this sentence?

   **a** submitted    **b** squandered    **c** unsettled    **d** written

Complete the word on the right so that it has an **OPPOSITE** meaning to the word on the left.

9  banish    | w | e |   |   |   |   | e |   |

10 loud     | i | n | a | u |   |   |   |   |

11 humble   | p |   |   | p |   | s |

12 poor     | p | r | o |   |   |   |   |   |

*Word Knowledge Tip!*

Look at the letters that have been given and use your knowledge of spellings. Is there a common prefix or suffix (in-, im-, re-, -ing, -ite, -ious, and so on)? Look at spelling strings to work out where the consonants and vowels are. If you don't know what to put down, make up some spelling strings that will form a logical word. This type of educated guess can be correct or, when you see the word, it can help you recall a word that is correct.

Find the missing three letters that complete these words. The three letters do not have to make a word. The same three letters are used for both words.

13  cu_____usly          luxu_____us

14  aggr_____ive         _____entials

15  dev_____ated         co_____line

16  exc_____ion          neighbo_____

Total  16

# Test 24

Find the missing three letters that complete these words. The three letters do not have to make a word. The same three letters are used for both words.

1  rest_____ant          thes_____us

2  po_____ity            burg_____ies

3  min_____m             s_____lator

4  i_____ngible          accide_____l

### Letter Tip!

Use your knowledge of letter combinations to help with these questions. You could also try covering up the word with your finger and then slowly reveal part of the word, forwards or backwards. This can make it easier to predict the word or to generate other words that might be related.

Select the **TWO** odd words out on each line. Select your answers by underlining **TWO** of the options **a–e**.

5  a race       b pace            c step       d jump       e stride

6  a defend     b protect         c shield     d medal      e ribbon

7  a trivial    b insignificant   c central    d crucial    e fundamental

8  a expose     b dodge           c evade      d avoid      e reveal

Underline the **ONE** word from options **a–e** that has the most **OPPOSITE** meaning to the word given.

9   meticulous   **a** imposing   **b** impossible   **c** impacting   **d** important   **e** imprecise

10   submissive   **a** resistant   **b** obedient   **c** weak   **d** understanding   **e** underused

11   vast   **a** vain   **b** massive   **c** small   **d** septic   **e** cast

12   successful   **a** peculiar   **b** absence   **c** rich   **d** ineffective   **e** evident

13   pretentious   **a** tasteless   **b** sour   **c** natural   **d** ornate   **e** fake

These sentences have been jumbled up and all have **ONE** extra word. Select the extra word in each of the sentences by underlining **ONE** word from options **a–e**.

14   we November winter celebrate of Bonfire fifth Night the on

   **a** celebrate   **b** fifth   **c** Night   **d** Bonfire   **e** winter

15   this our hibernating hedgehog a little lamb is in garden year

   **a** garden   **b** hedgehog   **c** hibernating   **d** lamb   **e** year

16   adverts are between of channels on programmes some television there

   **a** adverts   **b** channels   **c** of   **d** programmes   **e** television

17   carton sauce my raspberry fruit on put I ice some and cream

   **a** cream   **b** fruit   **c** raspberry   **d** sauce   **e** carton

18   rid the hours the she garden spent in house getting of weeds

   **a** garden   **b** hours   **c** house   **d** rid   **e** weeds

# Test 25

Find the three-letter word that is needed to complete each word so that each sentence makes sense. Underline the **TWO** answers needed from options **a–e**.

1  After her accident, the b_____age was app_____d to the wound.

   **a** eat    **b** and    **c** end    **d** lad    **e** lie

2  It was her tw_____th day on medi_____ion and she felt a little better.

   **a** all    **b** ale    **c** cat    **d** cot    **e** elf

3  We couldn't take much _____gage on the _____get airline.

   **a** bud    **b** bug    **c** log    **d** lug    **e** map

4  The holly b_____ies were enjoyed by a _____ge of birds.

   **a** run    **b** ran    **c** are    **d** err    **e** ode

5  The fields had jaunty s_____ecrows p_____ecting the newly sown seed.

   **a** car    **b** par    **c** hot    **d** rat    **e** rot

Select the **ONE** word on the right that has the most **SIMILAR** meaning to the word on the left. Underline the correct answer.

6  definite       **a** possibly    **b** unsure    **c** absolute    **d** potential    **e** brash

7  symbol         **a** sign        **b** drum      **c** blast       **d** time         **e** index

8  convenience    **a** difficulty  **b** ease      **c** solitary    **d** local        **e** portable

9  thorough       **a** exhaustive  **b** direct    **c** pressured   **d** slapdash     **e** by

10 waddle         **a** cuddle      **b** doddle    **c** muddle      **d** puddle       **e** toddle

The following sentences all have **ONE** word missing. Complete each sentence by selecting a word from options **a–e**. Underline the correct answer.

11  The games designers were trying to _____ a new and exciting app.

   **a** develop   **b** grow   **c** purchase   **d** apply   **e** repair

12  The _____ recorded the temperature on a regular basis.

   **a** microscope   **b** telescope   **c** thermometer   **d** microwave   **e** gauge

13  The teacher _____ how much work the choir had done, as their singing was superb.

   **a** appreciated   **b** disrespected   **c** suspected   **d** doubted   **e** assumed

14  The two little boys tried to _____ with walkie-talkie radios.

   **a** listen   **b** communicate   **c** act   **d** transfer   **e** exchange

> *Word Tip!*
>
> These questions can be easier when you look at the context of the sentence. What is it talking about? What words are associated with this context? You might then be able to cross out words that are definitely not appropriate.

Select the **TWO** odd words out on each line. Select your answers by underlining **TWO** of the options **a–e**.

15  **a** chunk   **b** lump   **c** slab   **d** pinch   **e** speck

16  **a** aromatic   **b** fragrant   **c** tasty   **d** flavoursome   **e** perfumed

17  **a** slug   **b** worm   **c** lizard   **d** tortoise   **e** crocodile

18  **a** star   **b** twinkle   **c** glisten   **d** glitter   **e** moon

*Time for a break! ★ Go to Puzzle Page 92 →*

# Test 26

Look at the words in the grid and then use them to answer the questions that follow.

| a fatigue | b antiquity | c creative | d painter | e amicable |
| f absurd | g yield | h smooth | i chaos | j arouse |
| k curious | l shiny | m artful | n ridiculous | o quarrel |
| p dispute | q wretched | r friendly | s custom | t lethargy |

1. Find **TWO SYNONYMS** for the word 'weariness'.

2. Find **TWO SYNONYMS** for the word 'sleek'.

3. Find **TWO ANTONYMS** for the word 'consent'.

4. Find **TWO ANTONYMS** for the word 'malicious'.

### Vocabulary Grid Tip!

Don't panic if you don't recognise some of the words. Begin with one word that you do know and see if you can match it up with another word. If not, is it an antonym or synonym for any question? If not, reject the word and try to find another.

Read the following sentences and answer the questions. Underline the most sensible word from options **a–d**.

'Smoking is prohibited for all inhabitants of the islands.'

5. What does the word 'prohibited' mean in this sentence?

    a allowed    b banned    c disliked    d enjoyed

6. What does the word 'inhabitants' mean in this sentence?

    a leaders    b homes    c visitors    d residents

'The besieged city had many fatalities from the earthquake.'

7  What does the word 'besieged' mean in this sentence?

   a beautiful    b historic    c surrounded    d fighting

8  What does the word 'fatalities' mean in this sentence?

   a deaths    b accidents    c births    d artefacts

---

Find the three-letter word that is needed to complete each word so that each sentence makes sense. Underline the answer needed from options **a–e**.

9  He had already con_____ed four bananas and a chocolate bar.

   a fed    b tan    c ten    d rum    e sum

10 The vacant house was so run-down and di_____idated.

   a did    b lap    c lip    d ran    e run

11 The g_____ent was embroidered with gold and silver thread.

   a lap    b ram    c arm    d rim    e alm

12 Marma_____e was easily made alongside other conserves.

   a due    b run    c lid    d ran    e lad

---

Select the **ONE** word on the right that has the most **SIMILAR** meaning to the word on the left. Underline the correct answer.

13 refuse    a accept    b except    c respect    d great    e rubbish

14 reliable    a dependable    b dreadful    c false    d dishonest    e decline

15 shoved    a nipped    b nudged    c nicked    d pushed    e sliced

16 singe    a burn    b tuneful    c sweet    d tinge    e dye

# Test 27

Select the **ONE** word on the right that has the most **SIMILAR** meaning to the word on the left. Underline the correct answer.

1  intangible    **a** ethereal    **b** real    **c** obvious    **d** tangy    **e** unappetising

2  liberty    **a** slavery    **b** restraint    **c** lightness    **d** freedom    **e** reading

3  oppress    **a** comfort    **b** obesity    **c** gladden    **d** cut    **e** persecute

4  rogue    **a** redden    **b** trickster    **c** comedian    **d** clown    **e** rural

5  bother    **a** heavy    **b** envy    **c** inconvenience    **d** ease    **e** comfortable

6  clot    **a** congeal    **b** hide    **c** liquid    **d** unwise    **e** reasonable

---

Complete the word on the right so that it has an **OPPOSITE** meaning to the word on the left.

7  traitor    l _ _ _ l s t

8  stretched    c _ m _ r _ s _ e _

9  guarded    u _ p _ o _ e _ t _ d

10  alert    l _ e _ _ a r _ _ c _

The following sentences all have **ONE** word missing. Complete each sentence by underlining a word from options **a–e**.

11  If anyone trips over the cable, we are _____, so make it safe.

   a immerse    b lying    c nimble    d liable    e insert

12  Breathe in quickly, then _____ slowly to get rid of nervousness.

   a exhale    b inhale    c hail    d extract    e extreme

13  The glass was blown and the window frame _____ from the fire.

   a possessed    b digested    c compacted    d charred    e resigned

14  If you _____ the dog, it makes her angry and she might bite you.

   a soothe    b harass    c please    d entertain    e feed

These sentences have been jumbled up and all have **ONE** extra word. Select the extra word in each of the sentences by underlining **ONE** word from options **a–e**.

15  shoes shorts pockets red belt new a and had her two

   a belt    b pockets    c red    d shoes    e shorts

16  was poster stuck painted the firmly brightly on the door the

   a door    b firmly    c poster    d stuck    e the

17  flowers beautifully full vase high scented of was the

   a beautifully    b flowers    c high    d scented    e vase

18  a bone dog down garden huge juicy the soil ran the with

   a dog    b juicy    c soil    d the    e ran

# Test 28

Find the three-letter word that is needed to complete each word so that each sentence makes sense. Underline the answer needed from options **a–e**.

1  We would love you to accom_____y us to the party.

   **a** man   **b** men   **c** pan   **d** pin   **e** sin

2  The teacher ack_____ledged the children's hard work.

   **a** war   **b** nil   **c** gnu   **d** new   **e** now

3  Please do not int_____upt me when I am talking.

   **a** are   **b** era   **c** err   **d** awe   **e** ere

4  The scientist was a pi_____er in genetic research.

   **a** and   **b** own   **c** eon   **d** one   **e** aim

The following sentences all have a short phrase missing. Complete each sentence by underlining a phrase from options **a–d**.

5  Chrissy loved to _____ on the River Dee.

   **a** sail a dingy     **b** sale a dingy
   **c** sail a dinghy    **d** sale a dinghy

6  He was so _____ what was in the locked drawer.

   **a** noisy he wandered   **b** noisy he wondered
   **c** nosy he wandered    **d** nosy he wondered

7  The lion crouched low so he could _____ before pouncing.

   **a** stair at his prey   **b** stare at his prey
   **c** stair at his pray   **d** stare at his pray

8  The _____ as it undertook an undercover operation.

   **a** convey was convert   **b** convey was covert
   **c** convoy was convert   **d** convoy was covert

Select the **ONE** word on the right that has the most **OPPOSITE** meaning to the word on the left. Underline the correct answer.

9  brutish     **a** feral      **b** wild      **c** mild      **d** bruised     **e** feline

10 despondent  **a** elated     **b** detailed  **c** gloomy    **d** gloating    **e** write

11 lucid       **a** clear      **b** obscure   **c** light     **d** weighty     **e** understandable

12 meld        **a** amalgamate **b** merge     **c** fuse      **d** twist       **e** separate

13 advance     **a** charge     **b** attack    **c** recede    **d** revise      **e** advise

14 grieve      **a** cry        **b** squeal    **c** queasy    **d** rejoice     **e** review

Select the **TWO** odd words out on each line. Select your answers by underlining **TWO** of the options **a–e**.

15 **a** opulent        **b** palatial    **c** basic      **d** sumptuous   **e** threadbare

16 **a** insubstantial  **b** fragile     **c** hefty      **d** weighty     **e** solid

17 **a** lilac          **b** lavender    **c** charcoal   **d** grey        **e** violet

18 **a** sleep          **b** drift       **c** sail       **d** snore       **e** glide

19 **a** template       **b** cupped      **c** outline    **d** outside     **e** specification

20 **a** tiptoe         **b** patter      **c** bawl       **d** howl        **e** bellow

*Time for a break!* ★ *Go to Puzzle Page 93* →   79

Total  20

# Test 29

Test time: 0   5   10 minutes

Find the missing letters that complete the word on the right so that it has an **OPPOSITE** meaning to the word on the left. Underline the correct answer from options **a–e**.

1  cheerfulness    m __ l __ n __ h __ l __

   **a** easuy   **b** aecuy   **c** eacoy   **d** aatoy   **e** eocoy

2  large    m __ n __ a __ u __ e

   **a** iitr   **b** ietr   **c** aetr   **d** eetr   **e** ootr

3  agreement    o __ __ o s __ __ __ o n

   **a** utilo   **b** utpri   **c** poiti   **d** rihre   **e** ppiti

4  pleasant    r __ p __ l __ i __ e

   **a** eatv   **b** eotv   **c** eusv   **d** eosv   **e** epan

5  simple    i n __ r __ c a __ __

   **a** tetu   **b** tite   **c** tane   **d** tise   **e** tote

Underline the **ONE** word from options **a–e** that has the most **SIMILAR** meaning to the word given.

6  agitated    **a** mature    **b** placid    **c** flustered    **d** calm    **e** sad

7  overt    **a** circular    **b** obvious    **c** unclear    **d** dense    **e** goodness

8  contrite    **a** extreme    **b** ballast    **c** rigid    **d** penitent    **e** gather

9  pallid    **a** flushed    **b** bright    **c** pale    **d** dark    **e** majestic

10  spirit    **a** wispy    **b** lucky    **c** person    **d** slippery    **e** energy

Select the **TWO** odd words out on each line. Select your answers by underlining **TWO** of the options **a–e**.

11  a partial   b section   c whole    d entire   e fragment

12  a nourish   b starve    c nurture  d kill     e encourage

13  a goods     b sell      c buy      d acquire  e purchase

14  a nimble    b supple    c agile    d taut     e tense

15  a condensed b contain   c short    d long     e brief

Select the **ONE** word on the right that has the most **OPPOSITE** meaning to the word on the left. Underline the correct answer.

16  discourage   a react    b reply     c motivate   d rotate    e dislocate

17  barely       a easily   b hardly    c softly     d roughly   e gently

18  excuse       a warrant  b forgive   c apologise  d punish    e trial

19  dormant      a sleepy   b sluggish  c immobile   d active    e rare

20  despise      a snub     b disgust   c adore      d defy      e detest

# Test 30

Select the **ONE** word on the right that has the most **OPPOSITE** meaning to the word on the left. Underline the correct answer.

1  pessimistic   **a** bleak   **b** charming   **c** optimistic   **d** simplistic   **e** proud

2  pinnacle   **a** culmination   **b** summit   **c** sharp   **d** base   **e** bind

3  abbreviate   **a** contract   **b** expand   **c** descend   **d** ascend   **e** resend

4  lowly   **a** common   **b** average   **c** lofty   **d** inferior   **e** gentle

5  encourage   **a** obstruct   **b** urge   **c** publicise   **d** locate   **e** lessen

6  ordinary   **a** ordered   **b** strips   **c** solidify   **d** common   **e** unique

These sentences have been jumbled up and all have **ONE** extra word. Underline the word that is not needed.

7  longer the shorter the wider were days getting and nights

8  leaves had sky autumn fallen the to ground the

9  there grass lots brown under tree were of conkers the

10  air there the was in the were bonfires smell of

11  monkeys their garden some spend forest home the in day all protecting

12  diamond seven colours there the distinct are of rainbow

Find the missing letters that complete the word on the right so that it has a **SIMILAR** meaning to the word on the left. Underline the correct answer from options **a–e**.

13  worry     a __ x __ e __ y

   **a** nir   **b** mit   **c** nit   **d** ner   **e** mir

14  endorse   r __ c __ m __ e __ d

   **a** oemn   **b** eamn   **c** eonm   **d** aenm   **e** eomn

15  tricky    c __ m __ l __ x

   **a** oee   **b** ope   **c** upe   **d** opi   **e** oce

16  disturb   i __ t __ r __ u __ t

   **a** nerp   **b** nepr   **c** terp   **d** rerp   **e** ners

17  spectacular   a __ t __ un __ in __

   **a** nrdg   **b** sogg   **c** sadg   **d** sodg   **e** sogd

Find the three-letter word that is needed to complete each word so that each sentence makes sense. Underline the answer needed from options **a–e**.

18  The ship had been torpe_____d during the war.

   **a** ear   **b** owe   **c** doe   **d** bee   **e** roe

19  The author had a real skill in describing his char_____ers.

   **a** ace   **b** act   **c** end   **d** err   **e** our

20  I had to int_____uce the school choir at our end of term concert.

   **a** rod   **b** red   **c** row   **d** too   **e** rue

21  He kept s_____bing his toe on the radiator.

   **a** had   **b** how   **c** tic   **d** toe   **e** tub

# Puzzle 1

## Word Search

There are 32 words hidden in this word search. Half of them have a similar meaning and the other half have an opposite meaning. Once you have found them, write the words with a similar meaning on the lines to the right, and the words with an opposite meaning on the lines below. The remaining letters spell out a hidden message reading from top left to bottom right.

```
S P E E C H L E S S O P R T I R
H M E A S U R E D S R E E H N E
O V E R W H E L M E D R L E T A
C O F M A S L S P R E P A R E D
K R L Y S T U R C E R L X M L Y
E G U S T U C E O N E E E L C
D A S T O N I S H E D X D T I O
E N T I U N D T E B W E O H G N
P I E F N E R R R A D D S O I F
R S R I D D C A E F A N P D B O
E E E E H E I N F L P U I L U
C D D D E X N T L T E Z C E N
I N S T A G G E R E D D Z A V D
S T A R T L E D O D C A L L C E
E F L A B B E R G A S T E D A D
C O N T R O L L E D B U D L L A
C O N F U S E D R C L E A R M Y
```

Hidden message: _____

# Puzzle 2

## Anagrams

Unscramble these words. Can you finish all four groups of eight words in just ten minutes?

### BIRDS

n b r i o  _____
r a t s l g i n  _____
r i b d a k l b c  _____
e n p o g i  _____
g l e e a  _____
l o w  _____
p i g a m e  _____
t i l t b u e  _____

### TREES

k a o  _____
n p e i  _____
r o m e a c y s  _____
n o r w a  _____
h a t w o n r h  _____
l e p a m  _____
r i c h b  _____
f r i  _____

### FLOWERS

s o r e  _____
y i l l  _____
p u t l i  _____
l i f o d f a d  _____
i s i r  _____
l u l e b l e b  _____
s a y i d  _____
y p p o p  _____

### METALS

d o g l  _____
s e v i l r  _____
o r i n  _____
i n c z  _____
u m i n i m a u l  _____
n i t  _____
z e r o n b  _____
c p p r e o  _____

# Puzzle 3

## Crossword

Can you fit the following words into the grid? The words are all descriptive of how strong or weak something is.

| healthy | robust | strong | powerful | vigorous |
|---------|--------|--------|----------|----------|
| dainty  | fragile | flimsy | delicate | weak |

86

# Puzzle 4 — Alphabet Categories

Find a word for each of these categories that begins with the same letter given at the top of the grid. The first one has been done as an example.

| CATEGORIES | B | C | D |
|---|---|---|---|
| Name | Ben | | |
| Occupation | builder | | |
| Adverb | badly | | |
| Animal | bear | | |
| Food | butter | | |
| Adjective | brave | | |

| CATEGORIES | F | G | H |
|---|---|---|---|
| Name | | | |
| Occupation | | | |
| Adverb | | | |
| Animal | | | |
| Food | | | |
| Adjective | | | |

| CATEGORIES | L | M | N |
|---|---|---|---|
| Name | | | |
| Occupation | | | |
| Adverb | | | |
| Animal | | | |
| Food | | | |
| Adjective | | | |

# Puzzle 5

## Word Grid

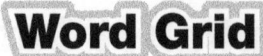

Place the words below into the grid so that each word fits. The letters in the shaded column will spell out another word. All of the words are related to controlling nature.

| | | | | |
|---|---|---|---|---|
| clipped | cropped | cultivated | cut | lopped |
| neat | pruned | snipped | tidied | trained |

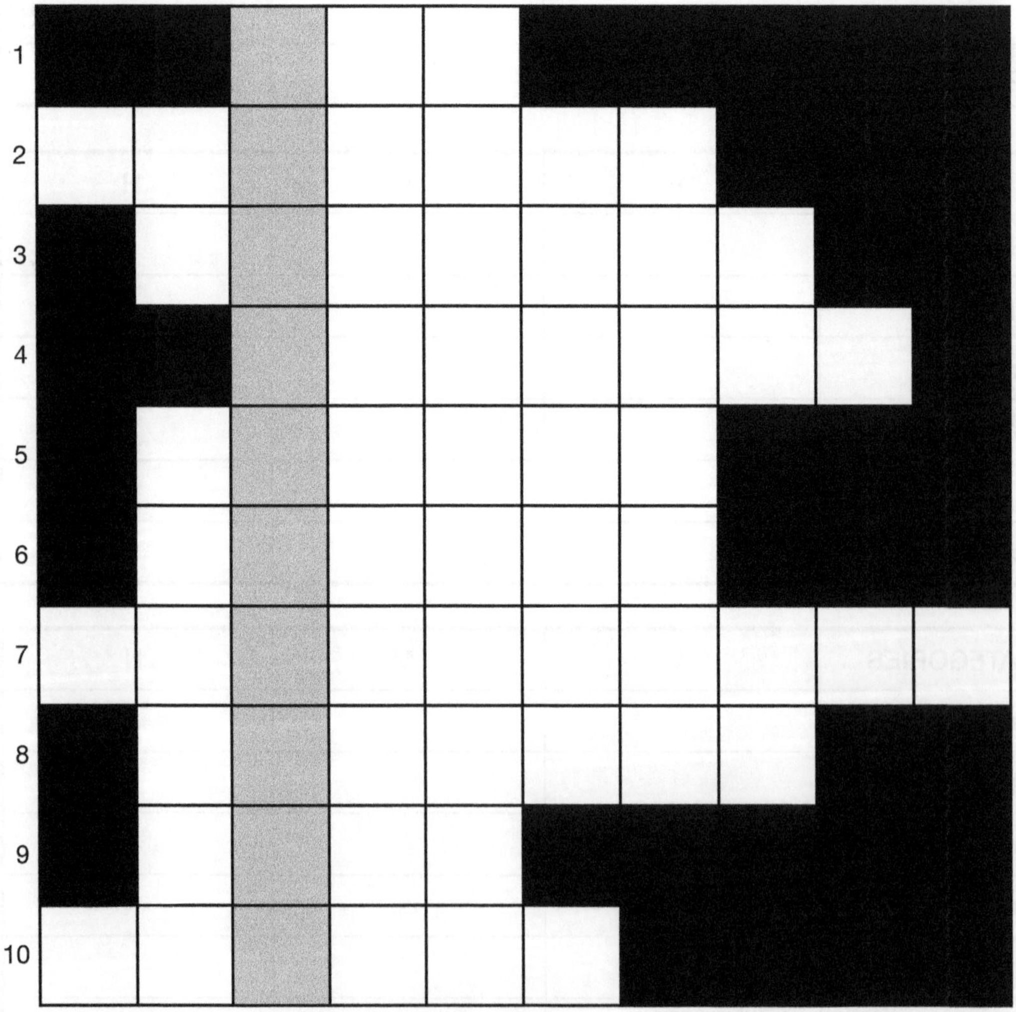

# Puzzle 6 — Add or Remove

All of the following words can have one letter added, or one letter removed, to make the name of a fish, bird, insect or mammal. Add or remove a letter and write the new word on the line.

**Fish**

code _____

place _____

reel _____

tun _____

trot _____

**Birds**

howl _____

sift _____

beagle _____

cow _____

ten _____

**Insects**

want _____

flay _____

been _____

was _____

lose _____

**Mammals**

cart _____

got _____

beard _____

rate _____

seep _____

# Puzzle 7 — Opposites

Here are 34 words that make 17 pairs of **antonyms**. Join each pair together with a line.

# Puzzle 8

## Linking Letters

Put these words in order so that the last letter of one word is the same as the first letter of the following word. The first pair has been done for you. All of the words are connected to positive and negative words.

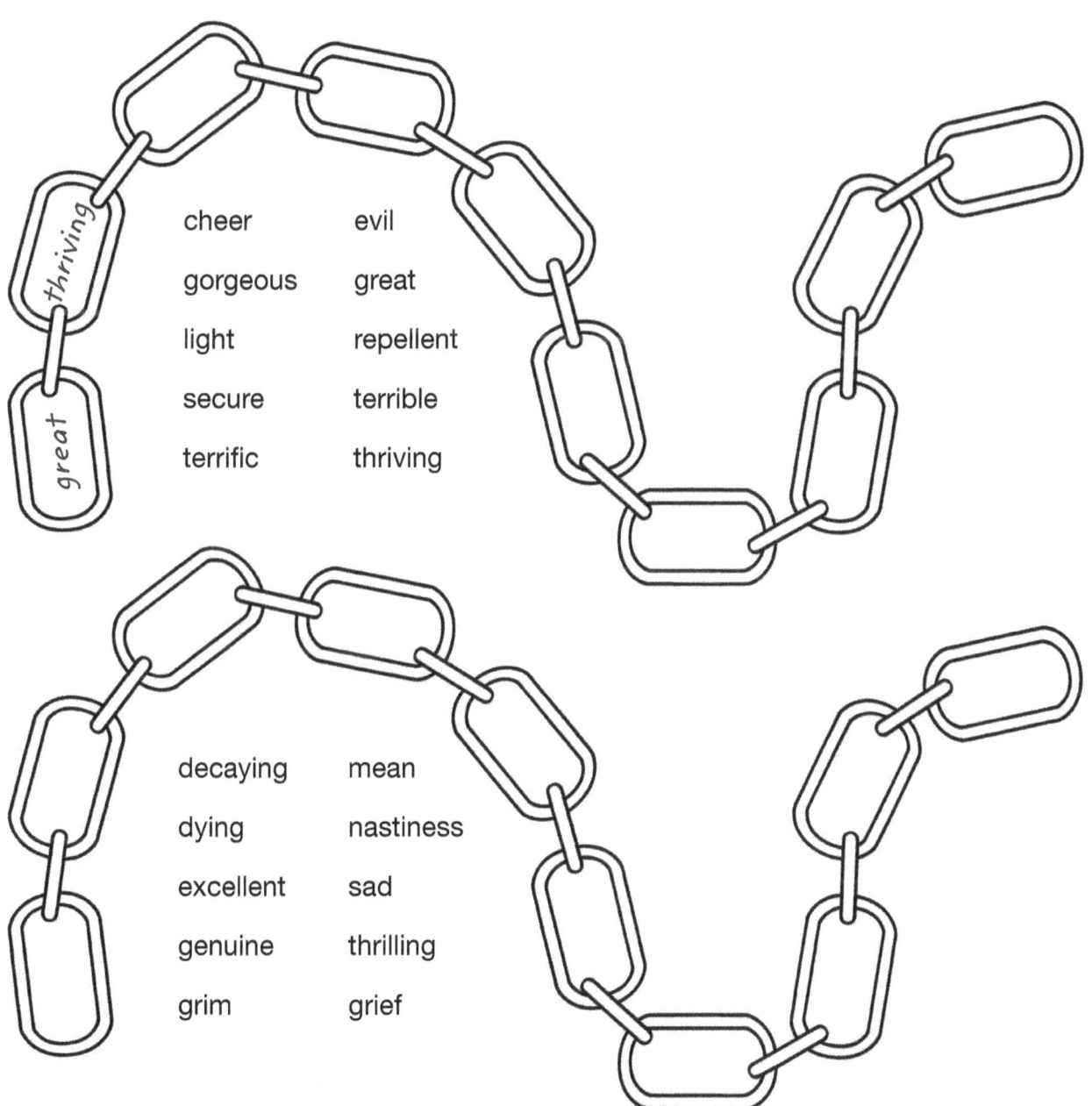

cheer
gorgeous
light
secure
terrific

evil
great
repellent
terrible
thriving

decaying
dying
excellent
genuine
grim

mean
nastiness
sad
thrilling
grief

Now that you have managed to link these words, why not try making your own linking words? You can choose any theme for the words. What about football teams, musical instruments, authors, funny words or names?

# Puzzle 9     Tricky Homophones

For each of the following words, there is one or more other word that sounds the same, but is spelt differently. Write a homophone beside each of the words below.

| | | |
|---|---|---|
| bawled _____ | bury _____ | due _____ |
| bawl _____ | discreet _____ | days _____ |
| carrot _____ | brooch _____ | oar _____ |
| cash _____ | throne _____ | bow _____ |
| bard _____ | board _____ | boy _____ |
| pray _____ | minor _____ | birth _____ |
| baron _____ | sole _____ | air _____ |
| principal _____ | bread _____ | draft _____ |
| dough _____ | dual _____ | censor _____ |
| maze _____ | mall _____ | manner _____ |
| medal _____ | taught _____ | bite _____ |
| sachet _____ | sear _____ | serf _____ |
| sheer _____ | slay _____ | naval _____ |
| steak _____ | sweet _____ | nay _____ |
| cymbal _____ | paws _____ | wail _____ |
| pedal _____ | Sunday _____ | wave _____ |

# Puzzle 10 — Odd Words Out

In each list of words, there are **TWO** words that do not fit with the other words. At the bottom of the page are four empty list boxes and the odd words out, when sorted, make these four lists with words that are connected. Find the odd words out and then place these words in the correct groups at the bottom of the page.

| List 1 | List 2 | List 3 | List 4 |
|---|---|---|---|
| partial | domed | rotten | sharp |
| whole | outside | stale | arched |
| fraction | exterior | curdled | rounded |
| segment | external | cuddled | pointed |
| total | shade | curved | spiked |

| List 5 | List 6 | List 7 | List 8 |
|---|---|---|---|
| dull | length | hugged | rejected |
| tint | full | tone | excluded |
| miserable | width | supported | embraced |
| hue | complete | aided | omitted |
| gloomy | height | helped | held |

| List 9 | List 10 | List 11 | List 12 |
|---|---|---|---|
| _____ | _____ | _____ | _____ |
| _____ | _____ | _____ | _____ |
| _____ | _____ | _____ | _____ |
| _____ | _____ | _____ | _____ |

# Puzzle 11 — Word Connections

In each 15-word grid below there are five sets of words, each with three words in them that are connected. For each grid, find all five sets of three words – but be careful as there are some words with more than one connection!

**1**

| reign | roasted | twist |
|---|---|---|
| French | oil | German |
| boiled | rain | grease |
| wind | Italian | fried |
| lubricate | turn | rein |

**2**

| ferocious | truthful | vigilant |
|---|---|---|
| gaudy | brutal | communicative |
| honest | wary | lurid |
| expressive | garish | candid |
| cautious | animated | vicious |

**3**

| ____lash | ____path | ____side |
|---|---|---|
| ____bell | ____lid | ____berry |
| ____food | ____print | ____flake |
| ____man | ____weed | ____step |
| ____plate | ____drop | ____ball |

*This one is trickier! Add the missing words to make compound words.*

94

# Key words

**antonym** A word that means the opposite of another word, for example *wet* and *dry* are a pair of antonyms.

**article** Articles are *the* (definite) and *a* or *an* (indefinite); articles are a type of determiner, for example *The children found a gold ring in the old jewellery box.*

**connected words** Many questions ask for connected words to be identified so that the 'odd word out' can be found. Remember to look for a connection to do with the following: a topic (for example *knife, fork* and *spoon* are connected as they are types of cutlery); the class of a word (for example *nourish, grow* and *feed* are connected as they are all verbs; watch out for verbs that can also be nouns, such as *feed*); synonyms or antonyms (*bury, conceal* and *cover* are connected as they are synonyms of the word *hide* and they are all antonyms of the word *reveal*).

**context** Other words in a sentence help us to understand an individual word, for example the word *wind* may be used in two different contexts (as a noun or a verb). We need the other words in the sentence to understand which meaning is being used: *The wind was blowing so hard that the trees were really bent over. I have to wind the alarm clock up each night.*

**homograph** A word that looks the same as another word when written, but has a different meaning. The words may also have different sounds when spoken, for example (1) *You are very kind. You bought the wrong kind of apple.* (2) *She wore a bow in her hair. We had to take a bow after the performance.*

**homonym** A word that looks the same as another word when written and sounds the same when spoken, but has a different meaning, for example *He hit the ball with the bat. We could see the bat flying at night.*

**homophone** A word that sounds like another but has a different meaning and may have a different spelling, for example *to, too* and *two* are all homophones.

**most similar / most opposite** Some questions are worded so that you find 'the most' similar or opposite. This is to encourage you to be precise in your choice of words. *Hot* appears to be an opposite word to *cool*, but it isn't really. The pairs of opposites are *boiling / freezing, hot / cold, warm / cool*. So there may be other words that appear to fit, but always look out for the 'most' similar or opposite.

**phrase** A group of words that are grammatically connected, for example *The patient was warned of adverse side effects.*

**synonym** A word that means the same as, or is similar to, another, for example *pretty, beautiful* and *attractive* are all synonyms.

**vocabulary** Words that are spoken, written and read, for example we talk about having a wide, extensive or broad vocabulary, which means the number of words that someone knows and understands.

# Progress chart

How did you do? Fill in your score below and shade in the corresponding boxes to compare your progress across the different tests.

| Test | Score |
|---|---|
| Test 1, p4 | ____/16 |
| Test 2, p6 | ____/20 |
| Test 3, p8 | ____/16 |
| Test 4, p10 | ____/16 |
| Test 5, p12 | ____/18 |
| Test 6, p14 | ____/16 |
| Test 7, p16 | ____/20 |
| Test 8, p18 | ____/20 |
| Test 9, p20 | ____/16 |
| Test 10, p22 | ____/20 |
| Test 11, p24 | ____/16 |
| Test 12, p26 | ____/20 |
| Test 13, p28 | ____/20 |
| Test 14, p30 | ____/20 |
| Test 15, p32 | ____/20 |
| Test 16, p34 | ____/18 |
| Test 17, p36 | ____/16 |
| Test 18, p38 | ____/16 |
| Test 19, p60 | ____/18 |
| Test 20, p62 | ____/20 |
| Test 21, p64 | ____/18 |
| Test 22, p66 | ____/16 |
| Test 23, p68 | ____/16 |
| Test 24, p70 | ____/18 |
| Test 25, p72 | ____/18 |
| Test 26, p74 | ____/16 |
| Test 27, p76 | ____/18 |
| Test 28, p78 | ____/20 |
| Test 29, p80 | ____/20 |
| Test 30, p82 | ____/21 |